Foundation Themes

Seasons

Liz Powlay

Text © 2003 Liz Powlay
© 2003 Scholastic Ltd

Designed using Adobe InDesign
Published by Scholastic Ltd
Villiers House
Clarendon Avenue
Leamington Spa
Warwickshire CV32 5PR

Visit our website at www.scholastic.co.uk

Printed by Belmont Press

1 2 3 4 5 6 7 8 9 0   3 4 5 6 7 8 9 0 1 2

British Library Cataloguing-in-Publication Data A catalogue record for
this book is available from the British Library.

ISBN 0-439-98464-5

Acknowledgements

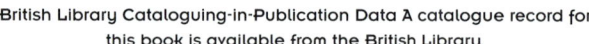

The publishers gratefully acknowledge permission to reproduce the
following copyright material:

Qualifications and Curriculum Authority for the use of extracts from the
QCA/DfEE document Curriculum Guidance for the Foundation Stage
© 2000 Qualifications and Curriculum Authority

Brenda Williams for 'Here comes the spring!', 'Busy, busy buzzing bee',
'Summer sunlight', 'Where is squirrel?', 'Ten white snowmen' and 'Sleepy,
sleepy bear' © 2003, Brenda Williams, all previously unpublished
(2003, Scholastic Ltd).

Sanchia Sewell for 'Please watch out!', 'Ask the birds', 'The waves at the
seaside', 'Did you ever see a spider?', 'Apple song' and 'Holly bushes
lovely to see' © 2003, Sanchia Sewell, all previously unpublished
(2003, Scholastic Ltd).

Every effort has been made to trace copyright holders and the publishers
apologise for any inadvertent omissions.

Author
Liz Powlay

Editor
Jane Bishop

Assistant Editor
Kate Element

Series Designer
Joy Monkhouse

Designer
Erik Ivens

Illustrations
Andy Robb/Beehive Illustration

Contents

Contents

Chapter 4 *continued...*

Photocopiables

Introduction

This book is one of a series of Foundation Themes books that covers a range of popular Early Years themes. It is written for all those working with three- to five-year-olds across a wide range of settings including Nursery and Reception teachers, pre-school leaders, nursery nurses and childminders. Each book in the series provides a variety of activities to support the Early Learning Goals and associated Stepping Stones as identified by the Qualifications and Curriculum Authority (QCA). The ideas can be used equally well with documents on pre-school education published for Wales, Scotland and Northern Ireland.

The books offer advice and guidance on all aspects of the Foundation Stage including planning, equal opportunities, special needs and assessment. In addition to a bank of activity ideas each book in the series includes suggestions for displays, circle time activities and photocopiable pages with activity sheets, new rhymes and songs. The themed activities form the main focus of each book and are aimed at an average four-year-old child with suggestions on how to offer support to younger children, to ensure they gain from the planned experiences, and ideas to extend each activity for older children.

Using a theme

Children learn best through experiences which are relevant and meaningful to them. By using a theme which has relevance to children and their experiences, practitioners can build upon the children's previous experiences and knowledge already acquired. This gives children opportunities to develop a broad range of concepts, skills and attitudes in all areas of the curriculum as identified by the six Areas of Learning in the Foundation Stage, while providing a coherent focus. A large theme such as 'Seasons' might be spread over a whole year, being dipped into on a regular basis, or it might be used to link events, such as harvest or even the children's interests, such as when there is a sudden fall of snow. The theme could be used for a few days to several weeks at a time. The 74 different activity ideas in this Foundation Themes book will ensure that the theme remains stimulating and interesting while providing plenty of hands-on experience.

Personal, social and emotional development

Communication, language and literacy

Mathematical development

Knowledge and understanding of the world

Physical development

Creative development

How to use this book

Providing a balance of learning opportunities for children is a demanding role and practitioners may often find that time is limited. This book provides quick and easy access to a wealth of ideas and inspiration. The activities are matched to the requirements of the Foundation Stage, each based on an Early Learning Goal (see logos in left panel) and clearly linked to an associated Stepping Stone, itself colour-coded to show whether the activity is at the simplest level (yellow), at a higher level (blue) or at the highest level (green), to match the colours used to show progression in the document *Curriculum Guidance for the Foundation Stage (QCA)*.

This book is divided into four chapters, one for each season.
♦ Chapter 1 explores the season of spring with advice on looking at the signs of spring through new life, changes to plants and spring weather.
♦ Chapter 2 makes the most of the summer weather with activities based around sun, sand, water, summer foods and holidays.
♦ Chapter 3 focuses on the changes that occur during autumn and uses the abundance of fruits, leaves and other autumn treasures for hands-on activities.
♦ Chapter 4 looks at the contrasting aspects of winter such as the warmth and excitement of fires, candlelight and winter markets and the cold and chill of snow, ice and life out of doors.

Each of these chapters can be used to provide a complete, pre-planned theme, as a mini-topic or dipped into for one-off ideas to support or enhance a practitioner's own ideas. Some of the activities are inter-changeable, for example those involving a study of the weather (see page 23) or cooking biscuits (see page 24) could be adapted for any of the seasons. This gives the practitioner scope to decide when it is appropriate to use the activity in their setting. Others can be prepared and resourced in advance, ready to produce at the ideal moment, such as the windy day activities (see page 54). Each season is further supported by ideas for display, circle time and through a range of photocopiable pages.

Photocopiable resources

Six new rhymes and six new songs are provided on pages 83 to 88. The songs are all set to well-known tunes that will be familiar to most practitioners and children. These resources are closely linked to the activities, often being used as a starting point or stimulus for further activity.

Photocopiable activity pages (pages 89 to 96) feature a wide range of resources including a game, a box template and picture sequencing that are closely linked to specific activities.

Links with home

Each activity gives suggestions for links with home so that parents and carers are encouraged to become involved in a variety of ways to support their children's learning. This will ensure that skills are developed both within the setting and at home.

Playing safe

Many of the activities in the book focus on children exploring the seasons through the use of their senses. It is therefore essential to check for any allergies or medical conditions before undertaking any activities that are not normally experienced on a day-to-day basis. Some of the activities take place away from the setting, in which case you will need to carry out a risk assessment prior to taking the children out, as well as informing parents or carers and obtaining their written permission.

Foundation Themes
Seasons

Planning

The experiences children in early years settings receive are dependent on practitioners offering a high quality learning environment, of which the planned curriculum is an essential part. Thought has to be given as to how children can be led forward in their learning, how these experiences are offered to the children and what they will benefit as a result.

Everyone, adult and child, learns by building upon what is already known and this important fact should be central to planning for progress in the Foundation Stage. It is also important to recognise that within a group of children there will be a wide range of developmental levels and that each child will have constantly changing needs, with learning progressing at differing rates in each area of the curriculum and at different times in their lives.

Experiences planned and offered to children should therefore build upon what is already known, be interesting and challenging, but not overwhelming or bewildering as this can lead to a loss of interest and motivation to learn.

As children learn in a variety of different ways planning should take this into account and include a range of approaches and teaching methods. There should be ample opportunities for play as this is the most effective way for young children to learn and use their new learning. Opportunities for children to learn through first-hand experiences, to develop their senses, to use imaginations, to develop and refine physical skills and to make sense of experiences through talking and listening, watching and trying, should be included.

Planning a theme

Planning a thematic approach, such as 'Seasons', allows the flexibility to cater for children's diverse and changing needs, enabling practitioners to offer a range of activities which constantly stimulate the children's learning. At the same time it can focus an individual child's learning and spark off trains of thought, giving them opportunities to set up their own activities, to develop their own learning and pursue a special interest at a pace and depth to suit their needs.

The activities provided in this book meet all six Areas of Learning described in *Curriculum Guidance for the Foundation Stage*. They cover a wide range of Early Learning Goals and Stepping Stones which are clearly identified on the activity pages, with each Stepping Stone being colour-coded to show the level. The planner on pages 10 and 11 shows the spread of cover among the six Areas of Learning and provides details of which clusters of Early Learning Goals are covered by each of the activities in this book. This enables a practitioner to plan a theme on 'Seasons' knowing that it will help to deliver the whole Foundation Stage curriculum in an interesting and focused way.

© Derek Cooknell

Each chapter looks at a season through many different types of activities. These could be introduced over a period of several weeks following a season as it progresses or used to dip into to support learning in a wider theme such as 'Our environment'.

To further assist with planning, sections at the end of each activity suggest other related activity ideas to extend the experience and consolidate the children's learning and how home links can support the child's learning. There are also theme links to suggest how the activity might link into another topic.

Planning is an on-going process and through the use of observation and assessment practitioners may find they need to adapt their plans to ensure that all children remain interested in what they are doing and that they are actively learning as they play.

Planning for equal opportunities

Children entering a setting will have come from a rich diversity of backgrounds and it is important that this is recognised and celebrated so that they and their families feel valued and welcome. A setting should aim to provide a safe, happy, relaxed environment free from discrimination and harassment, where children feel that their contributions are valued and respected and where there is no stereotyping by religion, race, gender or disability.

Planning for equal opportunities does not mean treating every child in the same way, but rather it is about ensuring that every child, whatever their need or inheritance, has a similar chance to take part in relevant opportunities and be set realistic and challenging expectations. Planning should also aim to help children respect and care for others, so everyone feels welcome and included. This should be an integral part of life in the setting.

The *Curriculum Guidance for the Foundation Stage* contains information and advice about planning to meet the diverse needs of all children. This includes the differing needs of boys and girls, children with special educational needs, those with disabilities, children with English as an additional language, those who are more able, and children from all social, cultural and religious backgrounds and those from different ethnic groups, such as refugees, asylum seekers and travellers and those children from diverse linguistic backgrounds.

© Erik Ivens

As a result of the SEN and Disability Act (2001), the Disability Discrimination Act has now been extended to cover education and this must be taken into account when planning activities for your group. Settings are required to make 'reasonable adjustments' to ensure that children with disabilities are not at a great disadvantage compared to their able-bodied peers. They must also ensure that they do not treat children with disabilities 'less favourably' because of their issues. The *Curriculum Guidance for the Foundation Stage* includes a specific section on planning for and supporting children with special educational needs and disabilities, helping practitioners ensure that they are able to provide them.

Practitioners should be aware of the content of various Acts covering the requirements of equal opportunities. These are the Sex Discrimination Act (1975), the Race Relations Act (1976) and the SEN and Disability Act (2001). It is also important to consider the requirements of the revised SEN Code of Practice during planning. This has a section covering the early years.

© Derek Cooknell

The activities within this book aim to meet the requirements set out in these documents and should therefore be suitable for most children. However some extra thought or adaptations will be needed in certain situations. For example, by providing extra adults and smaller groups for children with behaviour difficulties; considering the location for activities involving a walk to ensure it is fully accessible and changing the focus of an activity from looking to touch or smell to make it accessible to children with visual difficulties. It is important, therefore, that this is taken into account during the planning stage so that any adaptations, alternative materials and supporting adults are ready well in advance.

Long-, medium- and short-term planning

Effective and efficient planning is essential to all settings. Practitioners need to give thought to how they will promote children's learning, plan experiences, organise adult and children's time, resources and learning environment, and assess and evaluate both the children and activities. They also need to ensure that they offer a relevant, interesting and stimulating curriculum for all children, both long-term and on a day-to-day basis. All plans should be flexible enough to allow practitioners to adapt or introduce activities according to the developing and changing needs of the children in their group.

Long-term planning

Long-term plans can be used to take an overview of the themes and learning experiences and opportunities that will be offered to the children during the course of several weeks, a year or a child's time in the setting. They can be used to check that children are offered a wide-ranging, relevant curriculum.

They should include:
◆ a title for the theme
◆ any special events, planned activities or visits
◆ the six Areas of Learning.

Including the overall aims for the children's development in each area will help ensure the delivery of a broad and balanced curriculum.

Personal, social and emotional development

ELG Clusters	Activity	Page
Dispositions and attitudes	Winter market Good growing Celebration bells	62 75 78
Self-confidence and self-esteem	Harvest celebrations	46
Making relationships	Shadow games A giant spider's web	29 45
Behaviour and self-control	A caring spring Feed the birds	15 61
Self-care	Sandcastle challenge Time for bed	30 47
Sense of community	Celebrations tree	16

Creative development

ELG Clusters	Activity	Page
Exploring media and materials	Colours of spring Dyed eggs Butterflies Summer sun weaving Autumn art Ice art Winter landscapes	27 28 43 44 60 74 82
Music	Sounds of the sea	42
Imagination	Swirling snowstorm	73
Responding to experiences, and expressing and communicating ideas	Springtime corner puppets An autumn journey stick Autumn leaves	26 59 81

Foundation Themes

Physical development

ELG Clusters	Activity	Page
Movement	Floating bubbles Brrr… it's cold!	41 72
Sense of space	Spring cleaning	25
Health and bodily awareness	Making an autumn picnic	58
Using equipment	Summer games	40
Using tools and materials	A bag of spring biscuits Making a corn dolly Glitter, shine and sparkle	24 57 71

Foundation Themes Seasons

Communication, language and literacy

ELG Clusters	Activity	Page
Language for communication	Pack your bags	31
	The little red hen	48
	Candlelight poetry	64
	Harvest time memory game	77
Language for thinking	Spring showers	17
Linking sounds and letters	Winter rap	63
Reading	Apple and spice garlands	49
Writing	Miniature gardens	32
	Leaf litter confetti	50
Handwriting	Signs of spring	18

Seasons

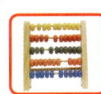

Mathematical development

ELG Clusters	Activity	Page
Numbers as labels and for counting	May flowers	20
	Fishing frenzy	33
	Apple tree bingo	51
Calculating	Sand treasure hunt	34
	Jolly snowmen	65
Shape, space and measures	Full to the brim	19
	Mary's summer garden	35
	Squirrel hide-and-seek	52
	Blazing fires	66
	Spring is here	79

Knowledge and understanding of the world

ELG Clusters	Activity	Page
Exploration and investigation	Changes diary	23
	Summer fruits and ice-cream	36
	Busy bees	37
	The apple challenge	53
	Catch the wind	54
	Hibernation holes	67
	Evergreen plants	69
	Sunlight's colours	80
Designing and making skills	Nest building challenge	21
	Tree treasure boxes	55
ICT	Hedgehog art	56
	Winter cave for a bear	70
Sense of time	Once upon a winter's day	68
Sense of place	Miniature pond play	22
	Seaside fun	39
Cultures/beliefs	A special day	38

Foundation Themes
Seasons

This could also include a brief outline of the associated Stepping Stones and Early Learning Goals to be covered.

The cross-curricular planner, on pages 10 and 11, shows how a theme such as 'Seasons' can cover many of the clusters and in turn Early Learning Goals and Stepping Stones. A planner like this is a useful tool in evaluating long-term planning and linking long-term plans to medium-term ones as it shows at a glance what is to be covered.

Medium-term plans

The next stage is to draw up medium-term plans that will build upon the outline ideas of the long-term plan and give more details. They are a clear, concise guide to when activities will take place, what they are, what is required and approaches to be used.

They should state:
♦ the different activities that will be offered
♦ the Early Learning Goals and Stepping Stones to be covered
♦ details of resources to be used
♦ suggestions for how children will be grouped
♦ adult roles and teaching or learning approaches
♦ how special needs are catered for and any adaptations that might be required
♦ opportunities for focusing assessment on particular areas of learning.

Short-term plans

The finest detail will be contained in your short-term plans which will focus on details of the planned activities, how they are to be carried out, what the children should learn and any assessment opportunities. They can also provide space to note next steps. They might cover a day at a time or a whole week.

These plans will detail:
♦ the different stages that take place for each activity
♦ whether an activity is to be child-led or adult initiated
♦ vocabulary to be used
♦ the organisation of the children, for example sat in a circle or in pairs or different activities for groups of children
♦ information relating to how children with differing needs are catered for
♦ specific resources needed
♦ the role of adults, including adult helpers
♦ links to other activities
♦ what is to be assessed
♦ space for next steps.

Because of their nature short-term plans can take into account changes that occur within the setting and the immediate needs of the children. In particular theme work that relies on the weather, such as Seasons, will have to be flexible depending on local conditions!

Short-term plans can also be modified due to any information that you gain about the children during assessment.

Although careful planning takes time, in the long run it should make life easier as a setting runs more smoothly when everyone knows what they are doing and why!

© Derek Cooknell

Assessment

Children enter early years settings having had a wide range of different experiences. They will have already learned a great deal and gained varying interests and skills. Through early assessment, observing, talking with and listening to children and discussions with parents and carers, practitioners can build up a picture of each child to assess what they already know, understand and can do.

Close observation of how children interact in different group situations is also vitally important, not only as part of personal, social and emotional development, but also for the future dynamics of groupings in the setting. All this information will then help the practitioner to plan, manage and appropriately resource activities and experiences. This will help to take children forward in their learning, ensuring that they all make progress and that any particular needs are detected early.

Building up a picture

Assessment is not a question of taking one look at a child and thinking that the job is done. It is an on-going process which, over time and together with supporting evidence, will build up a complete picture of the child. Assessment should take place on a daily basis so it becomes part and parcel of the daily routine, covering both the focussed, systematic, planned observations shown in a setting's planning as well as unplanned 'look at that!' observations.

Your most useful tool in the assessment process is the Curriculum Guidance for the Foundation Stage as it highlights each of the Stepping Stones that children need to progress through in order to achieve the Early Learning Goals by the end of the Foundation Stage. These Stepping Stones show the knowledge, skills, understanding and attitudes necessary for each Area of Learning in a hierarchical order where possible. Bear in mind however that not all children will conform to this sequence of learning and nor will they be at the same stage in all areas of the curriculum. Watching a child's progress against the Stepping Stones can help you identify any gaps in their learning and will enable you to adapt or amend planned activities to cater for each child.

Assessment can also be used to evaluate how well the setting is helping all children, for example, by assessing children's writing you might reveal a need to improve the appeal of the writing area so that children want to use it, to extend the range of materials or introduce appropriate stimuli to appeal to the differing needs of both boys and girls.

© Derek Cooknell

Gathering information

Observations used to assess how children are developing and progressing can take many forms and can change to suit different situations as they arise. Any information that you gather should be annotated to give background information on why it has been collected, if this is not obvious, and dated before being placed in the child's folder. This information can be gained through watching, talking with the children to find out more of what they are thinking or feeling, or working closely with an individual or group to gain an insight to what they know, understand and can do or need support with. It can be recorded by jotting down brief notes on paper or stickers or completing standard forms.

You can keep records of any models, constructions, role-play and outdoor activities through the selective use of photographs, video or audio tape. Remember to save samples of children's work or photocopy them if necessary.

Watching a child or group of children as they move around the setting, and how they choose between activities, can also help a practitioner to pinpoint areas or activities that certain children avoid or enjoy and this will highlight gaps in their experiences.

When assessing the development of children's skills it is important that evidence is gathered over a period of time. As children acquire new skills they need to learn how and when to use them. They also need opportunities to practise these skills many times in order to become confident and proficient in their use. Planning activities that allow the child to use these skills in a variety of situations will help show how a skill is developing.

Formal assessment

In addition to on-going assessment, practitioners will need to consider when and how to make formal assessments. One example of this is the individual Foundation Stage Profile document to be completed in the child's final term of the Foundation Stage to show the progress they have made.

Formal assessment may also take place when a child is causing concern or already has special educational needs. These assessments are used to gain precise and detailed information about a particular aspect of a child's development, in order to ensure that an effective and appropriate curriculum is in place to meet their needs.

For some children this might relate to one area such as behaviour or speech, for others it might involve several areas or revolve around physical access. In cases such as this, the types of information needed should be thought through in advance, with all those people involved with the child, to decide the best ways to gather and record the information and to monitor any progress the child makes.

© Derek Cooknell

Chapter 1

Spring

Celebrate the coming of spring with the seasonal ideas in this chapter. Discover how the warmer weather helps nature come back to life and offers opportunities for us to investigate the world around us with a range of cross curricular activities that will develop a range of skills.

A caring spring

Group size
Whole group introduction; small group activity.

What you need
Copy of the song 'Please watch out!' on the photocopiable sheet on page 86; pictures to show 'new life' such as new leaves or buds on plants and trees, bulbs, birds with their nests and animals with their young; large sheets of paper; writing materials; scissors; glue.

Preparation
Make an enlarged copy of 'Please watch out!'. Draw outlines on to the paper in shapes such as flowers, leaves, chicks and eggs. Cut out small slips of paper (smaller than the shapes).

Theme links
Changes
Nature
Our environment

What to do
Sing the song 'Please watch out!' with the children and look at the pictures you have gathered to show new life. Encourage the children to sing the song again and see if any of the pictures match the ideas mentioned.

Using the pictures to stimulate the children's ideas, talk about how spring signals the start of new growth: the plants and trees to grow new leaves, flowers unfurl, birds lay eggs and animals give birth to their young.

Invite the children to suggest ways in which we can help the plants, animals and birds, for example, by putting out food and nesting materials for the birds or not picking, pulling up or walking on the plants and flowers.

Working with small groups of children, write down their ideas on the small slips of paper and then read them together. Invite the children to select an outline (flower, leaf, chick, egg) and to cut out two identical shapes. Show them how to stick their idea on to one of the shapes and then glue the second shape over it to make a lift-up flap. Let the children use coloured pens and crayons to decorate the top piece of the shape. Display the completed shapes as a frieze around your room or link them together to make into a book to share.

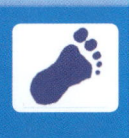

Stepping Stone
Show care and concern for others, for living things and the environment.

Early Learning Goal
Understand what is right, what is wrong, and why.

Support and extension
Offer support to younger children as they cut out the shapes or provide pre-cut shapes for them to use. Encourage older or more confident children to draw around a template or draw their own shapes. Invite them to write their ideas directly on to the shape or to trace over the writing.

Home partnership
Suggest to parents and carers that when they are outdoors with their children they invite the children to show them examples of new life in the environment.

Further ideas
♦ Go on a new life walk and invite parents and carers to accompany you.
♦ Make a decorative border for the 'Please watch out!' rhyme by asking the children to draw pictures of animals and plants to stick around the words.

Celebrations tree

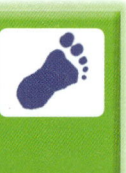
Group size
Whole group.

What you need
Large branches in bud from trees such as lilac or forsythia; bucket or large vase; compost or sand; paint; card; collage and craft materials; glue and spreaders; scissors; books and pictures about spring celebrations; music appropriate to the occasion.

Preparation
Make a celebration tree for a range of different special events and occasions by placing the branches in the bucket with the sand or compost and watering them. Ensure that it is stable. Collect together appropriate resources for the chosen occasion.

Theme links
Festivals
Memories
Our community

What to do
Sit in a circle and place the tree in the centre. Point out that the branches are looking bare. Ask the children to look closely at them. Can they see the buds? Explain that it is going to become a beautiful celebration tree, with the buds bursting open and branches covered in decorations that they are going to help make.

Talk about your chosen special event or occasion and make appropriate decorations to hang on the tree.

Suitable occasions might be:
♦ New baby being born: add the letters of the baby's name and pictures of him or her to the tree.
♦ First day of spring: ask the children to make spring flower garlands from tissue paper to drape around the branches.
♦ Easter: decorate card eggs, chicks and rabbits with collage materials and attach to the tree.
♦ May Day: make ribbon weavings to loop around the tree and add bells.
♦ Holi: decorate pre-cut bonfire shapes with powder paint and water and hang from the tree.

Invite the children to decorate the tree while you play some appropriate music to help set the scene. Encourage the children to talk about how they could celebrate the event.

Support and extension
Give younger children help with cutting and making the decorations, providing pre-cut shapes and templates. Invite older children to think of appropriate decorations to make, based on what they know or have learned about the celebration.

Home partnership
Invite parents and carers to let you know in advance of any special events or occasions that the group can share. Invite them to send in relevant pictures and artefacts or to share the event by visiting the group.

Further ideas
♦ Take photographs of the completed trees and mount them in a book for the children to talk about with each other.
♦ Share stories associated with different celebrations and act them out together.

Spring showers

Stepping Stone
Use talk, actions and objects to recall and relieve past experiences.

Early Learning Goal
Use talk to organise, sequence and clarify thinking, ideas, feelings and events.

Group size
Groups of eight children.

What you need
Outdoor area; tubs, buckets, boxes and lids made from different materials such as wood, plastic, metal, tin; umbrellas; waterproof clothing; wellington boots; camera; rainmakers; paper; mark-making materials; display table.

What to do
On a wet day look together out of your window or door at the rain. Invite the children to talk about what they can see. Ask them what they like to do on a rainy day. Have they ever played or been for a walk in the rain? What do they remember about it?

Invite them to put on waterproof clothing and wellington boots before going outside. Spend some time experiencing the rain and playing in it, feeling and catching raindrops on hands and faces and observing what is happening to the ground, buildings and windows. Look for puddles and compare the sizes and depths of them.

Talk about what they are doing and how they feel in the rain. Challenge them to find out what happens if they jump up and down on the ground, in a puddle or trace the pattern of drops on the window. Listen to the rain as it lands on different surfaces around the area. Give the children different items made from a range of materials, as well as umbrellas, to hold and listen to the noise the rain makes as it hits them. Invite the children to take photographs of the other children in the rain and the puddles and rain on different surfaces.

Back inside talk about the experience and draw pictures. Listen to the rainmakers and compare the sound with what the children heard outside – does it sound the same? Make a display with the wellington boots, waterproof clothing, the children's work, photographs and rainmakers. Encourage the children to look at and talk about the items displayed and to think back to their experiences in the rain.

Support and extension
Help younger children to put on the clothing. Ask older children to compare their experiences in the rain with those on a dry day. Let them talk about the differences and say which they enjoyed more and why.

Home partnership
Invite parents and carers to send in unwanted wet-day clothing which can be kept ready for children to use for outdoor play when it rains.

Further ideas
◆ Learn traditional rhymes about rain such as 'Incy Wincy Spider' or 'Rain, Rain Go Away'.
◆ Catch rain on raindrop-shaped card and sprinkle it lightly with powder paint. When it is dry ask the children to describe their rain shape, writing or scribing their description on to the card.

Theme links
Our environment
Water
Weather

Signs of spring

Early Learning Goal
Use a pencil and hold it effectively to form recognisable letters, most of which are correctly formed.

Group size
Whole group for song; small groups for activity.

What you need
Enlarged copy of the rhyme 'Here comes the spring!' on the photocopiable sheet on page 83; writing materials; paints; A4 and A5 paper, all to use landscape; card.

What to do
Say the rhyme 'Here comes the spring!' together, using the hand actions suggested. In a small group invite each child to select a sign of spring and to make a picture on A5 paper. When dry glue the pictures centrally on a piece of A4 paper.

For each picture lightly scribe the initial sound in pencil, on to the A4 paper, leaving a wide border around the edge. For example 'b' birds, 'f' flowers and 'n' nests. Encourage the children to follow the pencil outlines with their finger, ensuring correct letter formation. Invite them to use pens and pencils to trace over the outlines in different colours, helping them use a correct grip.

Make the paper into an opening pair of doors by folding in half and cutting from the crease to within 3cm of the open edge, 3cm in from the top and bottom edges. Open out the paper and cut along the central fold line. Glue along the edges of the paper and place over the corresponding picture. Join the pictures together to make a book.

Look at the book with the children and write the letters in the air. Open the doors, revealing the picture. Help them to think of a title for the book and write their names on the front cover.

Support and extension
Provide hand-over-hand support to younger children if needed when writing. For older children who are forming letters correctly, provide a few pencil outlines and encourage them to write the initial sounds themselves.

Home partnership
Send home a copy of the rhyme and ask parents and carers to look for the signs of spring mentioned during the coming weeks. Invite them to help their children to record these in a group diary.

Further ideas
♦ Decorate spring shapes with writing patterns for the children to trace.
♦ Paint spring pictures using letter shapes, for example a flower from circles, a tree from lines painted top to bottom.

Theme links
Change
Gardens and parks

Full to the brim

Stepping Stone
Use size language such as 'big' and 'little'.
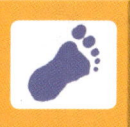

Early Learning Goal
Use language such as 'greater', 'smaller', 'heavier' or 'lighter' to compare quantities.

Group size
Six or eight children, working in pairs.

What you need
For each pair: variety of different sized seeds such as peas, beans, grass and conkers in bowls, sufficient for a pair of children to take a handful each; different sizes and shapes of containers such as a spoon, small film canister, plastic cup, yoghurt pot, clean foil take-away container; paper plate for each child.

What to do
Look at the range of seeds and talk about the differences in size. Ask the children to select one of each type and to arrange them in size order. Compare the size of the containers, asking the children to guess which will hold the most and the least peas. Find out together introducing mathematical language such as 'more', 'less', 'big', 'little', 'bigger' and 'smaller'. Repeat the activity, predicting and finding out which container will hold the least peas.

Invite the children to take a handful of seeds of their choice and to place them on their paper plate. Encourage them to predict whether their handful will fill the different containers before they try to do so. Ask the children to explain what they find out, again encouraging them to use correct mathematical language.
Repeat the activity using a different type of seed and then ask the children to try and arrange the containers in size order.

Support and extension
Support children by selecting two or three containers with obviously different sizes. Extend children by asking them to take a handful of seeds each and to try to guess who has the most before finding out. Let them decide whether to use a container, and if so which one, or whether to count them to work out the answer.

Home partnership
Encourage parents and carers to provide different containers for their children to use in the bath, the kitchen or the garden so they can make discoveries about capacity, size and weight while they play.

Further ideas
♦ Encourage the children to bring in different containers from home and make sets of them showing those that hold more than a yoghurt pot of peas and those that hold less.
♦ Fill identical small clear pots with lids with four different types of seeds. Ask the children to put them in order by how heavy they feel when they lift them up.

Theme links
Food
Measuring
Plants

May flowers

Group size
Six or eight children, working in pairs.

What you need
A selection of flowers or flower pictures; card; paint; glue; adhesive tape; thin plant canes; garden role-play items such as a table, display area, containers for flowers, play or real coins, order book made up of sheets of paper and plastic pockets in a ring binder, writing materials, tissue to wrap flowers, watering cans, plant pots, seeds and so on; the photocopiable sheet 'May flowers' on page 89.

Preparation
Set up a role-play garden centre.

What to do
Look at the flowers or pictures together. Encourage the children to help you count them in different ways, for example:
♦ how many flower heads
♦ how many red/ yellow/ blue ones
♦ how many stems or
♦ how many petals on different flowers?
    Ask the children to use card to make flowers and to fasten each one to a cane with clear tape. Arrange the flowers in containers in the garden centre.
    Show the children examples of bunches of flowers, for example, one red, three blue and two yellow, and record them by drawing pictures on paper. Place these examples in the order book.
    Encourage the children to play in the centre and invite them to place an order for flowers, either by selecting a page in the order book or by drawing what they would like. Help the assistants to make up the bunch, check it and wrap it ready for collection. Invite the customers to count the total number of flowers in their bunch on collection and to hand over a penny for each flower.

Support and extension
With younger children, initially limit the number of flowers in the bunch to three or five, prepare order pages for the children to use and provide flower shapes for the children to use to record their order. To extend the activity, place flowers in pots in a random arrangement and ask the children to count them. Challenge them to place them in sets by number or in number order.

Home partnership
Ask parents for magazine pictures of flowers to laminate and use for flower sorting and counting activities.

Further ideas
♦ Play the flower petal game on the photocopiable sheet 'May flowers'. Ask the children to take turns to roll a dice and colour in the part of the flower that matches.
♦ Make a flower catalogue. Collect or draw pictures of flowers. Write the numbers one to ten on consecutive pages of a book and ask the children to stick in the correct number of laminated flower pictures, using Blu-Tack.

Theme links
Gardens and parks
Plants
Shopping

Nest-building challenge

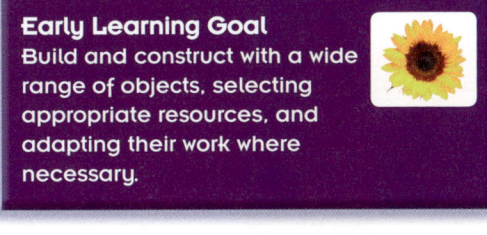

Stepping Stone
Construct with a purpose in mind, using a variety of resources.

Early Learning Goal
Build and construct with a wide range of objects, selecting appropriate resources, and adapting their work where necessary.

What to do
Invite the children to look closely at the nest pictures. Encourage them to try to describe how different nests are made: is it in layers, are materials woven in and out, what is the last layer made from? Explain that a nest is a bird's home, a place to lay their eggs and care for the chicks. Talk to the children about where birds build their nests and how they choose places that are safe from wind, rain, strong sun and predators such as other birds, cats and people. Help the children to learn the song 'Ask the birds' and ask what they think it would be like to build a nest.

Give the children a large protected area on which they can try to build birds nests, selecting from natural materials available and experimenting with the consistency of the mud and clay by adding water. Allow the children time to change the design of the nest over several sessions until they are happy with the final result. Encourage them to describe the changes they have made and why they made them.

Support and extension
Help younger children by providing a shallow container as a base on which to start building a nest. Extend the activity by challenging the children to design and build a nest to hold four chocolate eggs and two chicks.

Home partnership
Encourage parents and carers to make chocolate nests at home using melted chocolate and breakfast cereal. Ask them to experiment to find which cereal makes the best nest.

Further ideas
♦ Use tweezers to represent the birds beak and find out what it is like to build a nest like a bird.
♦ Use the tweezers in other activities, such as feeding cooked spaghetti 'worms' into a 'chick' made from a plastic bottle.
♦ Fill bags, made from wide mesh, with nesting materials and hang them outside to observe what the birds take.

Miniature pond play

Early Learning Goal
Observe, find out about and identify features in the place they live and the natural world.

Group size
Four children.

What you need
Water tray and washing-up bowls; water; greenish-brown paint; gravel; stones; rocks; plastic weed; plastic pond creatures and life-cycle sets such as newts, frogs, tadpoles, fish; small nets; large plastic tubs; simple reference books and picture keys; pictures of ponds, laminated; A2 paper and marker pen; A4 paper; mark-making materials.

What to do
Gather the children and ask them to describe a pond and what they might find in it. As the children share their ideas record them, helping them draw a pond on the A2 paper, using both words and pictures. Look at the picture and show the children the pond-making materials, bringing the items out as they describe the picture. Emphasise that ponds are dangerous places and they must only visit them when they are with a responsible adult. Invite them to make a safe miniature pond to play with.

Place all the materials in an accessible place and invite the children to make a small-world pond in the water tray or bowl, carefully adding the water (coloured with the greenish-brown paint) and arranging the pond environment. Encourage the children to look at the pond pictures if they need to find out where something goes. Invite the children to play in the finished ponds using the nets to fish out the creatures and adding to or altering the layout to improve the pond.

Support and extension
Provide ready-made pond bases with the water and gravel already added for younger children. Encourage them to add the other materials and creatures. After catching the creatures invite older children to place them in a dish and to use reference books to find out more about them.

Home partnership
Encourage parents and carers to take the children to visit a real pond in a park or garden centre. Ask them to talk to their child about staying safe near water.

Further ideas
♦ Make pond pictures using collage materials and different types of paper. Cover with Cellophane to create an under-water effect.
♦ Draw and name the pond creatures caught. Make the pictures into a laminated book for the children to use when playing in the small-world ponds.

Theme links
Homes
New life
Water

Foundation Themes
Seasons

Changes diary

Early Learning Goal
Look closely at similarities, differences, patterns and change.

Group size
Whole group.

What you need
Pictures of plants and trees in different seasons; outdoor area (short local walk with garden areas or park); camera; paper; writing materials; ready-made blank book to form a diary; adult helpers.

Preparation
Plan a short walk that will include a variety of plants for the children to observe closely for changes. This should include foliage and blossom appearing on trees and shrubs, bulbs growing and plants producing leaves and flowers.

Theme links
Change
Growth
Plants

What to do
Talk to the children about the plants and trees they see around their local area and in their gardens. Invite them to describe what they like about them, for example a tree that is covered in leaves to give shade or a rose that smells nice. Ask whether the plants and trees look like that now. Look at the pictures of the plants and help the children decide what time of year they were taken. Sort those that show plants like those around the setting at the present time.

Explain that everyone is going to help make a group diary, recording how plants change during the spring months, by visiting the same ones on a regular basis and drawing what they see and taking photographs.

Regularly visit the area and help the children record, through drawings and photographs, the changes they see. This might be every week or ten days depending on the weather and how quickly the plants change. Keep notes of the children's observations and scribe them back at the setting. With the children arrange them in the diary alongside the drawings and photographs.

Support and extension
Help younger children to concentrate on the changes around them by providing outlines of the larger trees and shrubs on which to record their findings. Challenge older children to sequence a second set of photographs showing how a plant has changed over the weeks.

Home partnership
Invite parents and carers to make a change diary with their children by selecting a local plant, tree or container to observe.

Further ideas
♦ Draw a map of the area and ask the children to record where the plants are while they are out on the walk.
♦ Plant seeds and bulbs and watch how they grow and change.

A bag of spring biscuits

Group size
Small groups.

What you need
Ingredients to make biscuits (see panel); baking trays; cutters in the shape of eggs, birds, flowers, rabbits or leaves; icing; cooking and hand-washing facilities; green and yellow tissue paper; scissors; ribbon; the photocopiable sheet 'Spring biscuits' on page 90.

Preparation
Ask for parents' permission to taste foods. Check for any allergies and dietary requirements.

What to do
Before starting ask the children to wash their hands. Explain that they are going to make some special spring biscuits to take home as a gift. Talk about the different cutter shapes and how these relate to spring.

Help the children to follow the recipe and mix the ingredients to make the biscuit dough, using the equipment carefully and safely. Invite the children to roll the mixture out to an even thickness and to make a selection of different-shaped biscuits using the cutters: check that the cutter is completely on the dough before they press down. Help the children lift the biscuits on to the baking sheet and then place them in the oven to bake them. When cool, invite the children to decorate the biscuits with icing. Leave to set.

Show the children how to make a gift wrapping by cutting two large squares of tissue paper, one yellow and one green, and to place them on top of each other so the corners of one piece are on the straight sides of the other piece. Help them to cut the squares and invite them to place their biscuits in the centre of the tissue and bring the corners together to make a bag, tying it up with ribbon.

Support and extension
Provide younger children with hand-over-hand support to cut out the biscuit shapes. Pre-cut the tissue or draw on squares for them to cut along. Invite older children to use card to make their own templates for their spring-shaped biscuits.

Home partnership
Encourage parents and carers to make biscuits at home with their children by attaching a copy of the biscuit recipe to the bag of biscuits.

Further ideas
◆ Cut spring shapes from ready-to-roll icing to decorate plain biscuits bought from the shop.
◆ Make a spring display with shapes cut from different colours of play-dough.
◆ Invite the children to cut out and sequence the biscuit-making pictures on the photocopiable sheet 'Spring biscuits'.

Spring biscuits
225g flour
120g margarine
100g sugar
1 egg
pinch of salt
grated rind of one orange
icing sugar and water to mix
◆ Sift flour and salt into a bowl.
◆ Rub in the margarine.
◆ Stir in the sugar and orange rind.
◆ Stir in the egg.
◆ Knead to make a firm dough.
◆ Roll out and cut out shapes.
◆ Bake for 10 minutes at 180°C, Gas Mark 4.

Theme links
Food
Gifts
Shapes

Spring cleaning

Group size
Whole group.

What you need
Copy of the action rhyme 'Spring Cleaning' by Sue Cowling in *The Works* chosen by Paul Cookson (Macmillan Children's Books) or make up a simple rhyme yourself to include sweeping floors, shaking rugs, cleaning windows, dusting; large space to move around in.

What to do

Read the rhyme to the group and ask them to talk about how their homes are cleaned. Introduce the idea of how we give a house a spring-clean to greet the warmer, lighter days. Explain that in earlier times this was necessary to remove all the dirt and dust caused by the open fires that were used to keep each room warm through the winter, before cleaner types of heating, such as radiators and storage heaters were available.

Re-read the rhyme and invite the children to suggest actions for each idea and to show them to the rest of the group. Encourage all the children to try the actions and then to make up one of their own. Ask the children to show this action to a friend who should then copy it. Invite the children to move around the space trying out the actions high up and low down and to the sides without touching another child. Repeat this for the different cleaning actions mentioned in the rhyme.

When the children are confident with the actions to the rhyme, slowly re-read the rhyme and ask them to act it out, using a sequence of actions to mime the different cleaning actions.

Support and extension

For younger children, model cleaning actions for them to copy. Invite older children to think of other cleaning jobs that are not included in the rhyme, such as polishing a table, cleaning the bath and hoovering carpets, and to think of suitable actions for them.

Home partnership

Ask parents and carers to encourage their children to help with suitable cleaning jobs around the home.

Further ideas

♦ Make certificates to give to children when they have helped in the home or kept their things tidy for a week.
♦ Have a spring-clean of the setting, with the children helping to wash toys, dust books and polish tables.
♦ Using suitable music develop a 'Spring cleaning' dance by linking together two or three actions from the rhyme and repeating them around a large open space.

Theme links
Homes
Keeping healthy
Rhymes

Springtime corner puppets

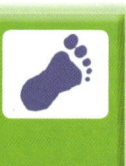

Group size
Small groups.

What you need
Card; templates of birds, flowers, chicks, trees; scissors; paint; glue; assorted collage materials; 15cm lengths of thin dowel; adhesive tape; spring music such as Vivaldi, *Four seasons* 'Spring'; pictures of spring; garden netting; green crêpe paper streamers; paper leaf shapes; tissue paper blossom; containers with flowers, bulbs and bursting twigs.

Preparation
Make a spring corner by securing the netting across the ceiling and arranging the crêpe paper streamers, leaves and blossom on the netting and walls. Display the other resources. Make four different stick puppets (see 'What to do') and hide them among the display.

What to do
Play the spring music as the children walk into the area. Encourage them to sit quietly and listen. Invite the children to say what the music is 'telling' them and how it makes them feel. Ask what they can see in the 'spring' area, including spotting the puppets. With the music in the background, use the puppets to tell the children about spring, each one explaining what happens to them. For example, for the tree: leaves start to grow and blossom appears, insects visit the flowers and birds nest in the branches.

Invite the children to make their own stick puppets to illustrate the signs of spring. Help them to cut out a card shape by drawing around a template and then provide paint and collage materials for them to decorate it. Leave these to dry before fastening a piece of dowel to the back with adhesive tape.

Play the music again and encourage the children to make the puppets 'dance' to show their happiness at spring arriving.

Support and extension
For younger children pre-cut shapes from card and hide them in the spring display for children to find and decorate. Help a group of older children to make up a short play to show the other children what happens during spring.

Home partnership
Invite parents and carers to view the puppets and spring area.

Further ideas
♦ Invite the children to make up their own spring music. Record it to use with the puppets.
♦ Let the children dance to spring music.

Theme links
Materials
Puppets

Colours of spring

Group size
Four children.

What you need
Bought samples of spring gift wrap and cards; green, yellow, blue, red and white paint; dishes or saucers; potatoes and sponges cut into flower and leaf shapes; folded cards in pastel colours; white, green and yellow tissue paper; sheets of greaseproof paper.

What to do
Look at the gift wrap and cards with the children, highlighting the choice of fresh spring colours such as green and yellow or pastel shades. Talk about the designs. Are they all over the sheets, random or repeating patterns? How many colours are used? Explain to the children that they are going to make their own cards and gift wrap to take home.

Invite the children to mix paints to make the colours they would like to use. Show them how to take white paint and gradually mix a little of the darker colour into it until they reach the shade they want. Demonstrate how to make a careful print using the sponges or potatoes, holding them still as they print. Encourage the children to mix and use their own paint colours to make potato and sponge print patterns on to a card and tissue and greaseproof paper, thinking about the design and position of the prints. Leave to dry flat.

When dry help the children to write a greeting such as 'Enjoy the warm spring days' or 'Happy spring-time' inside the card. Scribe if appropriate. Help them to wrap up a gift using their paper. This could be a picture the child has painted, biscuits they have made, or bulbs they have grown.

Support and extension
For younger children provide ready-mixed colours. Give hand-over-hand support when making the prints. With older children, cut sections out of gift wrap or cards, glue on to a piece of paper and ask children to complete the missing parts or make up a design based on the cut out piece.

Home partnership
Send home the card and wrapped gift with a note explaining that the children mixed the paint and printed the card and gift wrap themselves.

Further ideas
♦ Mix paint and find out how many shades of green or yellow can be made. Match them to colours around the setting.
♦ Use a computer paint program and design a card or gift wrap pattern.

Theme links
Colour
Gifts and giving
Patterns

Foundation Themes
Seasons

Dyed eggs

Group size
Small group.

Preparation
Ask for parents' permission to taste foods and check for any allergies and dietary requirements.

What you need
Examples or pictures of dyed and decorated eggs, wrapped up in boxes, labelled 'open carefully'; fresh eggs – one per child; a large quantity of onion skins; sewing thread; legs from clean, old tights; saucepan; cooker; 3cm rings of card cut from kitchen roll tubes; paint; glue; sequins.

What to do
Invite the children to guess what is inside the boxes before opening them. Pass around the eggs encouraging children to look carefully at them, describing the colours. Explain that they are going to decorate fresh eggs in a special way that has been used for generations, especially during celebrations about new life and Easter. Tell the children that these were placed in a bowl on a table as a decoration before being eaten.

Show the children the eggs, explaining that they are fresh, not cooked and will break if they are dropped. Demonstrate to the children how to wrap the egg up in onion skins and to bind it with the thread to secure the skins. Help the children to carefully wrap up their eggs. Place them inside the legs of the tights and then in the pan. Cover with cold water and boil them for 30 minutes. Leave to cool in the water overnight.

The next day, ask the children to gently unwrap the eggs and discover what has happened. The eggs should be marbled in orange, yellow and red colours. Invite the children to each make a decorated stand for their eggs by decorating a ring of cardboard with paint and sequins. Send the eggs home with a note explaining that they are dyed with onion skins and are edible.

Support and extension
For younger children use a dab of safe glue to help hold the skins in place. Give help with the wrapping and tying. Let older children experiment using beetroot, dandelion leaves and red cabbage to wrap around the eggs before they are boiled.

Home partnership
Ask parents to help collect the onion skins needed to dye the eggs. Invite any who have some decorated eggs to come in and show them to the children.

Further ideas
♦ Make papier-mâché eggs using a small balloon as a base.
♦ Decorate paper-craft eggs and then thread them to make a mobile.

Theme links
Eggs
Celebrations

Chapter 2

Summer

Make the most of the long summer days with this range of cross-curricular activities. Encourage the children to find out how under the warmth of the summer sun the flowers and gardens thrive, we enjoy holidays at the seaside and have fun playing outside in the fresh air .

Group size
Ten children.

What you need
Sunny day; outdoor area.

Shadow games

What to do
On a sunny day take the children outside. Encourage them to stand still and look around and to tell you all the things they can see in the sunshine. Talk about how everything has a shadow. Ask the children to try and run away from their shadow. Invite the children to play games with their shadows such as run and freeze, making the largest shadow, the smallest and the most weird shaped ones. Can they move so their shadow is in front of them and then behind?

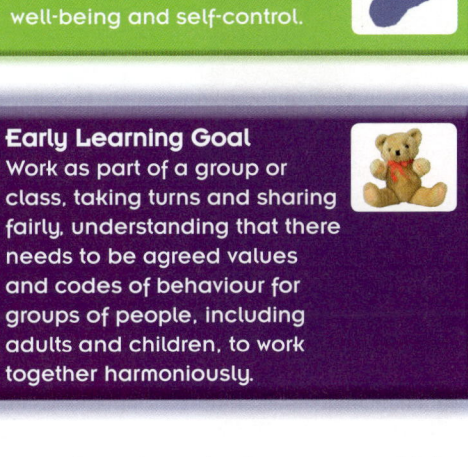

Stepping Stone
Value and contribute to own well-being and self-control.

Early Learning Goal
Work as part of a group or class, taking turns and sharing fairly, understanding that there needs to be agreed values and codes of behaviour for groups of people, including adults and children, to work together harmoniously.

Explain to the children that they are going to play shadow games in which they have to work together and take turns. Introduce shadow games which involve careful positioning and thought, for example can the children arrange themselves so everyone is standing on the head of someone's shadow? Ask the children to make a line so a foot shadow touches a hand shadow or so each person's hand shadow looks like it is tickling the tummy of another shadow.

Finish the session by playing shadow tig with two people chasing the others and trying to catch the shadows with their own. If the shadows touch they must shout 'freeze'. Let them swap catchers when two children are caught.

Support and extension
For younger children work with groups of five children, taking part in the simpler activities. Extend the activity by placing a teddy on the ground and inviting the children to try and make a ring of shadows around it without actually touching anyone, so it looks as though everyone is holding hands.

Home partnership
Ask parents and carers to look for shadows around the home and when outside.

Further ideas
♦ Take turns to match photographs of shadows to actual objects.
♦ Work together to make a shadow puppet play for a favourite story.

Theme links
Light and dark
Our environment

Foundation Themes
Seasons

Sandcastle challenge

Group size
Small groups.

What you need
Damp sand in a deep tray or pit; different-sized plastic containers such as buckets, tubs, cups and yoghurt pots; spades; paper; plant sticks; tape; scissors; fine sandpaper; card; glue; laminating materials; smiley face stickers.

Preparation
Make some sample sandcastle designs by cutting out pieces of sand paper to match the containers you have available. Arrange each one on a separate card and laminate them. Make paper flags with smiley faces on and tape them to the sticks.

What to do
Invite the children to play freely in the sand tray for several minutes with just the spades. Talk to them about what they are doing. Introduce some of the containers and ask them what they could make with them, again encouraging exploratory play. Discuss what the children make for example, who has made the largest pie or the tallest tower.

Show the children the sandcastle design cards and talk about how the sandcastles could be made. Challenge the children to make the different designs, explaining that an adult will return shortly to admire them and give out smiley faces if they can make them on their own. Encourage the children to find the containers independently or by asking another child to help or share theirs.

On returning, admire the sandcastles and give out the flags for the children to place on each castle as a finishing touch. Talk about how they made the castles. Praise their attempts at being independent and give each child a sticker.

Support and extension
Support younger children by giving them three or four carefully selected containers to make sandcastles, using corresponding design cards. Ask older children to make a sandcastle and record it using the sandpaper. They could then challenge a friend to make it.

Home partnership
Explain that the setting is encouraging independence and ask parents and carers to set simple tasks at home to support this, for example asking the children to put their own shoes away.

Further ideas
♦ Hide shells, stones and other natural materials in a sand tray for children to find and use to make a picture.
♦ Add small-world figures to the sand tray to encourage children to enjoy independent and imaginative play.

Theme links
Buildings
Seaside

Foundation
Themes
Seasons

Pack your bags

Stepping Stone
Initiate conversation, attend to and take account of what others say, and use talk to resolve disagreements.

Early Learning Goal
Interact with others, negotiating plans and activities and taking turns in conversation.

What to do
Sit together in a circle around the adult and watch as they struggle to put all the items in the bag. Encourage the children to talk about what is happening and why the person is packing a suitcase, contributing ideas on what the person should do. Establish that this person is going on a summer holiday and perhaps only some of these items are needed. Invite the children to suggest items which are essential, listening to and sharing ideas.

Explain to the children that this person is not the only one who finds it difficult to decide what to take on holiday. Read the story of *Little Bean's Holiday* where the main character wants to take every toy with her on holiday.

Invite small groups to work together to pack a bag for a holiday that they choose for Little Bean. Encourage them to select a particular type of holiday and to choose suitable items, ensuring they fit in the suitcase. After packing look at the contents together and ask the children to tell you why they chose these items.

Support and extension
For younger children break the activity up and provide fewer items to select from. Help them to select a type of holiday. For older children give a group a picture from a holiday brochure and ask them to pack items for that holiday.

Home partnership
Ask parents and carers to help children choose a postcard while they are on holiday to bring back and talk about.

Further ideas
◆ Work in pairs to sequence a picture story of a holiday.
◆ Set up a holiday role-play area for the children to visit with their packed bags.

Theme links
Journeys
Stories

Miniature gardens

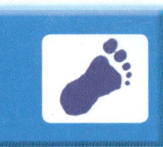
Early Learning Goal
Attempt writing for different purposes, using features of different forms such as lists, stories and instructions.

Group size
Small groups.

What you need
Local garden or park to visit; writing materials; paper; foil dishes; compost; gravel; seeds such as grass, cress and small flowers (such as alyssum); tiny plug plants; small pieces of wood; glue; foil; the photocopiable sheet 'Make your own garden' on page 91 enlarged to A3; word and picture cards of materials used.

What to do

Visit the garden or park and look at what is growing and what the children like best. Talk about how it is full of life, growth and colour during the summer.

Back in the setting ask the children to make pictures of the garden labelling their favourite features, ask an adult to scribe captions for their pictures.

Explain to the children that they are going to make a miniature summer garden of their own which will need looking after. Help the children fill the dish with compost and to add grass seed to one area to make a lawn. Carefully make paths and patio areas using the gravel, then plant the plug plants, cress and flower seeds to make flower borders. Invite the children to add features such as ponds using foil or seats made from wood.

Encourage the children to record their finished garden on the photocopiable sheet drawing on the features then adding labels, either by using the word processor with supporting pictures or by copying from the word cards.

Work as a group to write a list of things needed to make the gardens and a set of simple instructions. Display with a selection of the children's pictures, recording sheets and miniature gardens.

Support and extension

Give one-to-one support when younger children are making their gardens. Cut out the pictures on the side of the photocopiable sheet and help them to glue them on to their copy of the garden in the relevant places. Encourage older children to keep a diary to record the changes that occur in their garden each week.

Home partnership

Send home some seeds, such as nasturtium or marigold, for the children to plant. Ask parents and carers to talk about the changes that occur with their children.

Further ideas

♦ Place plants in containers. Make name labels for them.
♦ Write shopping lists and make posters for a role-play garden centre.
♦ Keep a weekly plant diary, adding different forms of writing.

Theme links
Gardens
Growth

Foundation Themes
Seasons

Fishing frenzy

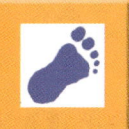

Group size
Small groups.

What you need
The rhyme 'One, two, three, four, five' in *This Little Puffin* compiled by Elizabeth Matterson (Puffin); blue sheet; large shallow cardboard box; paints; coloured card; large paper clips; magnets attached to string; wellington boots; waterproof coats; buckets.

Preparation
Use the cardboard box to make a boat, painting on details. Cut fish shapes from card in different colours and place numerals one to five on some and different dot patterns one to five on others. Secure a paper clip to each fish. Cut out some card boot, bottle and crab shapes for bad catches.

What to do
Arrange the blue sheet on the floor to represent the water and place the cardboard-box boat on top. Scatter the fish and other shapes around the boat. Sit near the boat and sing the rhyme 'One, two, three, four, five' with the children. Invite the children to dress up in the waterproof clothing and to go fishing from the boat. Encourage them to use the lines to fish among the shapes to try and catch the fish and place what they catch in their buckets. Ask questions as they make a catch, such as 'How many fish do you think you have now?', 'Have you caught more fish or more bad catches?' and 'How many spots has this fish?'.

When all the fish have been caught ask the children to count how many are in their bucket. Can they find out who caught the most red, green or blue ones and how many there are altogether? Play games with the fish such as asking the children to place five fish in number order, then take one away and ask 'Which is missing?'. Alternatively take a numeral fish and find its spotty partner or vice versa.

Support and extension
Invite younger children to catch three fish each and to sort the catch by colour. Extend the activity by asking older children to share the fish so each child has the same number of fish and some of each colour.

Home partnership
Encourage parents and carers to sing number rhymes with their children.

Further ideas
♦ Ask the children to find how many different ways they can arrange five fish or boats in two ponds.
♦ Put out differing amounts of waterproof clothing and ask 'How many children can fish?'.

Theme links
Counting rhymes
Transport
Water

Sand treasure hunt

Group size
Up to four children.

What you need
Sand tray with dry sand; spades; small items or toys such as pennies, cars, animals, shells (ten of each); card, laminator; wipe-off marker pen.

Preparation
Make a set of cards showing a picture of each item, one for each child and laminate them. Hide the small items or toys in the sand.

What to do

Talk about playing on the beach or in a sand-pit on a warm summer's day. Invite the children to dig in the sand tray to find some hidden treasure. Encourage the children to tell you what the different types of treasure are and to arrange it in sets. Count the items at regular intervals and pose problems for the children such as 'How many will there be if you find one more?' 'How many will there be if I put one back?', 'I thought I buried five pennies, have they all been found yet?' or 'How many are still buried?'.

Invite the children to bury the found treasure in the sand. Show the children the cards and give them one each. Use the marker pen to write on the cards the number of each item to be found, to suit each child's ability. Encourage the children to dig out an item, and place it in their set, sorting and counting their treasure and saying whether they have it all or too much, and whether they think some is still buried or if some needs to be re-buried so the other children can claim them.

When all the treasure is found, re-number the cards and play again.

Support and extension

Hide just three items for younger children to find. Extend the activity by secretly removing an item and see if the children can work out which one is missing.

Home partnership

Encourage parents and carers to use mathematical language while they play with their children, for example with cars, crayons, or cooking. For example 'two cars and one more, that's three cars'.

Further ideas

♦ Hide shells in the sand an d ask the children to find a given number and then make a set with one less or more.
♦ Bury cubes in the sand. Use a sand timer and challenge the children to build a tower in pairs. Compare the finished towers.
♦ Fill a shallow tray with fine gravel. Give the children pots of differing sizes and challenge them to find out which pot holds the most.

Theme links
Seaside
Toy and games

Mary's summer garden

Stepping Stone
Show interest by sustained construction activity or by talking about shapes or arrangements.

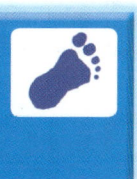

Early Learning Goal
Talk about, recognise and recreate simple patterns.

What to do
Share the rhyme 'Mary, Mary, quite contrary' with the children, encouraging them to join in. Talk about how the rhyme describes a garden with flowers growing in rows and invite the children to tell you about any gardens they have seen filled with summer flowers. Encourage them to think about how the flowers were arranged, using the pictures to help them develop the language of shape and arrangement.

Look at the large Clip Art pictures and ask the children to tell you which part of the rhyme each one might be linked to. Explain that they can use smaller copies of these pictures to make a Mary's garden of their own. Make a sample garden together, demonstrating how to make a sponge print path on a sheet of paper, then inviting the children to each choose a flower or shell to put in the borders and beds.

Invite the children to make their own garden pictures, printing the paths first. Encourage them to think about and describe the type of path such as 'straight', 'wiggly', 'round' or 'curving' and to name the shapes used. While the pictures are drying help them cut out the flowers and shells. Invite them to arrange these on the picture first, gluing them down when they are happy with the arrangement.

Support and extension
Encourage younger children to talk about the arrangements of flowers they make. Pre-cut the majority of the pictures. Invite older children to make repeating patterns with the rows of flowers.

Home partnership
Ask parents and carers to help their children make a flower garden collage using pictures cut from old magazines or seed catalogues.

Further ideas
♦ Draw shaped flowerbeds such as triangles or circles to be filled with flowers.
♦ Make flowers from construction materials such as straws and magnetic or slot-together plastic shapes.
♦ Make a large, paper flower chain, with a repeating pattern of size or colour.

Theme links
Patterns
Plants
Shapes

Summer fruits and ice-cream

Stepping Stone
Talk about what is seen and what is happening.
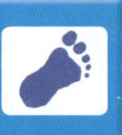

Early Learning Goal
Look closely at similarities, differences, patterns and change.

Group size
Small groups.

What you need
Summer berries such as strawberries, raspberries, redcurrants, dessert gooseberries; sugar; safe knives; chopping boards; small bowls; teaspoons; ingredients for ice-cream (see panel); cup measures; two small zip-lock bags; extra large size zip-lock bag.

Ice-cream
1 cup whole milk
½ cup double cream
4 teaspoons icing sugar
½ teaspoon vanilla extract
4 cups of small ice cubes
2 tablespoons coarse salt.

Preparation
Ask for parents' permission to taste foods and check for any allergies and dietary requirements.

What to do
Sit around a table and invite the children to look carefully at the summer berries, exploring the colour, smell, taste, finding the seeds and looking for juice on their fingers. Talk about summer being the time of year when these special berries grow as the sun and warm weather are needed to ripen them.

Help the children to chop up the berries they like and mix them with a sprinkle of sugar in a small bowl. Label and put these to one side.

Talk about eating ice-creams on hot summer days and invite the children to make some. Put one small zip-lock bag inside the other and help the children to measure out 1 cup milk, ½ cup cream, 4 teaspoons icing sugar, ½ teaspoon vanilla extract and to place it inside the inner bag. Seal both bags securely, removing excess air. Add ice and salt to larger bag and place the smaller bags inside and seal firmly. Let the children pass around the bags. Encourage them to shake and turn the bag, mixing together the ingredients. Watch and talk about the changes that occur. The ice-cream will be soft and ready to eat in five to ten minutes.

Invite the children to share the ice-cream out into the bowls of fruit and eat it, watching what happens as it melts and how the juice colours the ice-cream.

Support and extension
Give hand-over-hand support to younger children while they are chopping and measuring. Extend the activity by asking older children to make observational drawings of the fruit.

Home partnership
Ask parents and carers to point out summer fruits when they are shopping or to visit 'pick-your-own' outlets with their children.

Further ideas
♦ Try other simple summer fruits recipes such as summer pudding.
♦ Sort 'soft' and 'hard' fruits.

Theme links
Food
Fruit

Busy bees

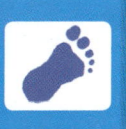

Early Learning Goal
Find out about, and identify, some features of living things, objects and events they observe.

Group size
Small groups.

What you need
A garden area with flowers and bees; foods and products made with honey, including honeycomb; books and photographs of bees; dead bees (from windowsills) placed in sealed clear plastic boxes; hand lenses; copy of the rhyme 'Busy, busy, buzzing bee' on the photocopiable sheet on page 83; teaspoons; cling-film; wall filler; water; yoghurt pots; yellow and black paint; bristles from a new broom; strong black thread.

Preparation
Ask for parents' permission to taste honey and check for any allergies and dietary requirements.

What to do

Sit together and pass around the clear plastic boxes with the bees in, hand lenses and photographs for the children to study. Talk about how bees collect nectar from the summer flowers to turn into honey, which is their winter food. Introduce the rhyme and use it as a stimulus for further discussion, getting additional information from the books. Show the children the honey products and smell, touch and taste them.

Explain to the children that you are going outside to observe bees visiting flowers. Encourage them to sit quietly, watching the bees move from flower to flower.

Afterwards, invite the children to make plaster bees, to hang up above the honey products. Help them cover a teaspoon in cling film and place a thread trailing out of the centre for hanging the finished bee. Place a small amount of filler in a yoghurt pot. Add water until a very thick mixture is made and place it in a mound, like a bee's body, on the covered teaspoon. Add six legs and antenna from the brush bristles. Leave to set, then paint.

Make a display of the bees, books and honey products, together with the children's work.

Support and extension

Give younger children extra adult support to ensure they get the most from observing the bees. Extend the activity by making a large collage of a bee and flowers, based on the children's observations.

Home partnership

Encourage parents and carers to send in items for the display. Suggest they visit a park looking for bees visiting the flowers.

Further ideas

◆ Invite a beekeeper to visit and talk to the children.
◆ Find out which flowers attract bees, plant some in a quiet area where the children can watch.

Theme links
Food
Gardens
Insects

Foundation
Themes
Seasons

A special day

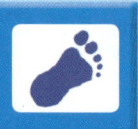

Group size
Whole group.

What you need
Mementoes of a special occasion or visit made by an adult in the group in summer; extra adults; letters inviting families to send in mementoes and to join a circle time; display space; camera.

What to do
Gather together in a circle and show the mementoes. Explain why these items are special, describing to the children the events to which they relate. Invite them to carefully pass them around the circle. Encourage the children to comment on them and ask questions.

Talk about the summer having better weather and longer days, so families are more likely to go on special days out such as a picnic, a trip to the beach, to weddings or other celebrations, to meet up with other family members and to go on holiday.

Divide into smaller groups with an adult in each and encourage the children to share the special times they remember with the other people in the circle.

Plan a series of short special circle times and send home letters, giving the date and time, to invite parents and carers to join you. Ask for the children to bring in photographs and mementoes of special occasions, visits or holidays. Encourage the children and a parent or other supporting adult to talk about the things they have brought in and the event associated with it.

Take a photograph of the children with their mementoes and help them to place it and the mementoes on display, scribing an information card with the child. Invite them to add their name and to draw a relevant picture.

Support and extension
With younger children use a circle of just four or five children. Encourage older children to make a booklet about their special event, placing the photograph taken above on the front cover.

Home partnership
Invite parents and carers to help their child decide on a special event, what to talk about and bring in.

Further ideas
♦ Look at books that show life in any countries that have been mentioned by the children as holiday destinations. Play appropriate music and try some foods eaten in these countries.
♦ Go on a simple group outing, take photographs and collect mementoes to hang up as a mobile.
♦ Invite visitors to come and show the children artefacts connected with celebrations from a range of faiths.

Theme links
Families
Journeys

Seaside fun

Stepping Stone
Show an interest in the world in which they live.
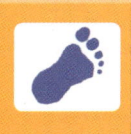

Early Learning Goal
Observe, find out about and identify features in the place they live and the natural world.

Group size
Whole group, in pairs.

What you need
Outdoor area; blue fabric; paddling pools with salty water containing drift wood, plastic boats, sea creatures, shells and rocks; sand-coloured fabric; sand pits with wet, dry and pebbly sand; spades; sieves; moulds; nets; buckets; deck chairs; parasols; towels; beach clothes; sun-hats; baskets; picnic play-food; the photocopiable sheet 'Beside the sea' on page 92.

Preparation
Check for children who have eczema or contact dermatitis.

What to do
Talk to the children about the seaside and why people go there in the summer. Think about what is found there and what you can do. Invite the children to help set up a seaside play area with a sandy beach area, using the 'sandy' fabric and sand trays, and a wet sea area with the blue fabric and paddling pools. Place the deck chairs and parasols along the 'beach'. Arrange the beach clothes, buckets, spades, nets, towels, baskets and picnic food near by.

Invite the children to visit the seaside, encouraging them to put on the clothes, pack up a picnic and collect together nets, buckets and spades. Allow the children time for free exploratory play and to have a 'picnic' before introducing activities, such as a sandcastle competition, a boat race, timed fishing game to catch three different types and building a rock pool.

Follow up the seaside play by handing out copies of the photocopiable sheet and inviting the children to fill in the spaces on the pictures by thinking about their experiences and drawing in the items.

Answers: 1 sail, 2 sun, 3 spade, 4 creatures in the rock pool, 5 bucket, shell, rock, sandcastle or seaweed.

Support and extension
Support children in completing their activity sheet, suggesting ideas for what might be in the missing parts, including some incorrect ones. Invite older children to paint two contrasting pictures, one showing something found at the seaside and the other of something near their home or setting.

Home partnership
Send home copies of seaside rhymes, poems and tongue twisters for parents and carers to share with their children.

Further ideas
♦ Use recyclable materials to make a small-world beach scene.
♦ Hide pictures linked to the seaside and other places in the sand. Sort the 'seaside' ones into a bucket.
♦ Display postcards of beaches that the children have visited.

Theme links
At the sea
Natural materials

Foundation **Themes**
Seasons

Summer games

Group size
Individuals and pairs.

What you need
Outdoor area; child's skittles and hoopla game; empty plastic drinks bottles; sand; empty, sealed washing powder boxes; card tubes; thick cardboard; scissors; glue; paint; coloured paper; assorted stickers; assorted balls; quoits; star-shaped card badges; smiley face stickers, in different colours.

What to do
Talk about summer fêtes and the games the children have seen there or games they have tried on holiday which involve throwing or rolling skills. Explain that people play these games because they want to win a prize if they are successful. Show the children the examples of the hoopla game and skittles and ask for volunteers to have a go, encouraging and praising careful, accurate attempts.

Invite groups of children to make a game to try out their skills, using the materials available. For example:
♦ encourage them to make skittles from large fizzy drinks bottles decorated with brightly-coloured stickers
♦ show them how to make a hoopla from decorated card tubes, the ends cut and splayed out and secured to thick cardboard or plastic bottles, partly filled with sand and stood up
♦ invite them to stack decorated boxes, as a wall or tower, ready to knock down.

When the games are completed set them up in the outside area and encourage the children to try their luck. Encourage them to have several attempts, carefully aiming and rolling, kicking or throwing the ball or quoit. Reward the children's efforts with a smiley sticker on one point of their star badge. Invite the children to try the other games to collect a full set of stickers.

Support and extension
Provide large sponge balls for younger children to use. Encourage older children to hit balls with bats or sticks at a target on the ground or around obstacles.

Home partnership
Encourage parents and carers to play games with their children, both outside with balls and inside throwing rolled-up socks into a bucket.

Further ideas
♦ Cover old balls in paint. Place them on paper inside a hoop and push the balls from side to side to make a pattern.
♦ Explore the different ways a beanbag can be moved for example dropped, thrown, slid, patted or kicked.

Theme links
Myself
Toys and games

Floating bubbles

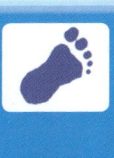
Group size
Ten children.

What you need
Bubble mixture and blowers; large area, preferably outside.

What to do
Talk with the children about how some things are more fun to do in the summer, than at other times of year, for example eating ice lollies or walking barefoot on the grass. Mime these actions and ask the children to think of other ideas and to mime actions for these too.

Show the children the bubbles and ask them to think about why these seem more special when they are used outside in summer: the sun catches them and they look like rainbows, it is not a problem if they are accidentally spilt. Blow some bubbles towards groups of three children and ask them to each catch one, without touching another child.

Explain that lots more bubbles are going to be blown and invite the children to chase after them, catching and popping them, again without touching another child. Play games to discover who had to run the furthest and jump the highest to catch a bubble. Show the children how to blow bubbles for each other to catch.

Ask the children to sit down while you blow some bubbles, watching how they move. Invite the children to imagine they are bubbles moving around the area, being blown from a blower, gradually getting larger and larger until free and then floating and bobbing in the breeze, until finally they burst into a gentle spray of water. Talk about the movements the children create and invite them to show the others in the group.

Support and extension
Place stable containers of bubble mixture on a flat surface for younger children to access. Extend the activity for older children by asking them to make groups of three, holding hands in a circle. Encourage them to float and drift around like bubbles, joining together to form one large bubble which eventually goes pop.

Home partnership
Encourage parents and carers to let the children have bubble baths and to provide assorted containers for bubble play.

Further ideas
♦ Place hoops on the ground to represent bubbles. Travel around the hoops and on the shout 'pop', jump in a hoop.
♦ Add paint to bubble mixture and blow a mound of coloured bubbles and take prints of them.

Theme links
Air
Water

Sounds of the sea

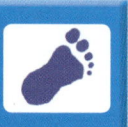

Group size
Whole group.

What you need
Copy of the song 'The waves at the seaside' on the photocopiable sheet on page 87; CD player; CD of atmospheric sea music; empty plastic fizzy drinks bottles; funnels; water; blue food colouring; glitter; sand; gravel; shells; small pebbles.

What to do
Invite the children to curl up on the floor and play the sea music CD. Ask them to imagine it is a hot summer's day and they are lying on the beach listening to the sounds around them. What would they hear? Afterwards talk about the noise waves make, the tide on the beach, waves on rocks, lapping, sloshing, splashing and gulls shrieking in the air.

Share the song on the photocopiable page with the children, singing it through a couple of times and encouraging them to join in. Explain that they are going to make sea-sounds instruments to use with the song and sea music.

Add blue colouring to the water. Invite the children to choose a plastic bottle, place a funnel in the top and add some glitter, blue water and one of the 'noise' materials such as sand, gravel, shells or small pebbles. Ensure the bottles are securely fastened. Show the children how to tip the bottles back and forth and to roll them on the floor to make sloshing sea sounds. Explore how to make loud raging wave sounds, sloshing and splashing in the sea type noises and creeping, lapping water sounds.

Use the instruments to accompany the song and with the CD of sea music.

Support and extension
Include wide-necked plastic jars for younger children needing support to fill them more easily. Encourage older children to make instruments using boxes, tins, tubes and the 'noise' materials, but no water. Explore the different types of sounds these can make.

Home partnership
Encourage families to send in materials such as sand, gravel or shells for the children to use in the instruments.

Further ideas
◆ Use the song and sea sound instruments as a stimulus for making a simple dance.
◆ Draw wave patterns of different sizes on to strips of paper. Join them together in a line and use the instruments to play the pattern of the waves: the smaller the wave the quieter the sound.

Theme links
Senses
Songs and rhymes
Water

Foundation
Themes
Seasons

Butterflies

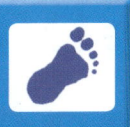
Group size
Individuals.

What you need
Pictures of butterflies; thick paper kitchen towel or large dry baby wipes; butterfly template; scissors; thick water-based felt and marker pens, water; droppers; display board covered with blue paper.

What to do
Talk with the children about butterflies only being seen in the summer when there is plenty of nectar in the flowers for them to feed on, and fresh leaves to lay eggs on, ready for the caterpillars to eat when they hatch. Look at the pictures of the butterflies and observe the colours and types of patterns on their wings.

Invite the children to each make their own butterfly by drawing around the template with the felt pens on to kitchen paper towel or a baby wipe and cutting out the butterfly shape. Explain to the children that they need to draw large patterns on one half of the butterfly with thick water-based marker pens, trying to copy the patterns they have seen in the pictures. Show them how to fold the decorated side of the paper over so the colour is inside, but it forms the top layer. Invite them to carefully drip water over them, watching the colours spread and merge as the paper gets wet. Unfold gently and leave to dry.

Display the butterflies against the blue on the display board as if they are flying in the air.

Support and extension
Support younger children by pre-cutting the butterfly shapes. Invite older children to make a butterfly to their own design. Show them how to make a symmetrical butterfly by folding the paper in half, drawing half the shape and cutting through both thicknesses.

Home partnership
Suggest that parents and carers point out any butterflies they see in the local area to their children.

Further ideas
◆ Make a repeating butterfly pattern by printing with half a large apple dipped in paint, adding features with pen.
◆ Decorate half of a butterfly-shaped piece of paper with painted shapes, fold over, press, open up and dry. Decorate the paint shapes with felt pen and pastel designs.
◆ Decorate butterfly shapes with wax crayons and add a colour wash.

Theme links
Colours
Insects
Shapes

Summer sun weaving

Group size
Whole group, in pairs.

What you need
Pictures of the sun, at different times of the day; copy of the rhyme 'Summer sunlight' on the photocopiable sheet on page 84; assorted yellow, orange and gold materials such as textiles, plastic, ribbons, foil, paper, wool, cut into long strips; curtain rings; beads; garden netting with 2cm hole, stretched and secured to a hoop.

What to do

Talk as a group about the sun, and find out what the children know about it already. Tell them that it is a star, far away and explain that it takes the Earth a year to travel all the way around the sun. The Earth spins round every 24 hours giving us day and night but because the Earth spins at an angle, it is hotter and brighter in the summer when we are closer to the sun. Remind the children that it is dangerous to look directly at the sun, and like all hot things, it can burn. Share the 'Summer sunlight' rhyme with the children and look at the pictures, talking about the different colours they can see. Identify hot, sunny colours around the setting.

Show the children the collection of materials, curtain rings, beads and the hoop and invite them to make a sun using weaving techniques. Demonstrate how to weave materials in and out of the netting holes. Encourage pairs of children to weave their chosen materials through the holes, working in both directions leaving lengths overlapping the hoop to represent the rays. As they weave suggest they thread on some rings and beads. Explain that the materials can overlap each other, passing through the same holes.

When the weaving is complete, hang up next to a copy of the rhyme, together with the children's sun drawings, paintings and other works of art.

Support and extension

Support younger children by helping them decide whether the materials should weave up or down next. Extend the activity by showing children how to tie on items, like sequins or baubles to give a 3-D effect.

Home partnership

Invite parents and carers to send in materials in sun colours to use in the weaving.

Further ideas

♦ Make sunrise or sunset pictures by painting a background and adding a pasta sun, sprayed silver or gold.
♦ Weave strips of tissue paper in sun colours around the rays of a sun, made from evenly spaced cuts from the edge to near the centre of a circle of card.

Theme links
Colours
Day and night

Chapter 3

Autumn

The variety of activities contained within this chapter provide an exciting selection of autumnal fun ideas. Use the abundant natural resources of leaves, acorns, conkers and fruit to explore the season. Find out how animals prepare for shorter days and hold some harvest celebrations.

A giant spider's web

Group size
Ten children.

What you need
Floor area protected by a plastic sheet; black paper; white or silver paint; saucer; marble; pencil; Plasticine; white or silver wool; black card; glue; scissors; black pipe-cleaners; black fur fabric or tissue paper; wobbly eyes; copy of the song 'Did you ever see a spider?' on the photocopiable sheet on page 87; pictures of spider's webs.

Preparation
Cut out a large circular piece of black paper around which all the children can sit. Pour some of the white or silver paint on to the saucer.

Theme links
Homes
Minibeasts

What to do
Sit the children in a circle around the black paper. Look at the pictures of webs and encourage the children to talk about what they can see. Sing the song together and consider how hard the spider works to make such a beautiful thing.

Explain to the children that they are going to take turns to make their own beautiful web. Place a marble in the white or silver paint and roll it across the paper from child to child. Take turns, placing the marble back in the paint before each roll, until a criss-cross web appears on the paper. Next make holes along some of the radiating arms of the 'web' by pushing a pencil through the paper into the Plasticine. Invite the children to weave wool through the holes to make the rings of the web.

Together, make spiders to sit on the web by cutting out circles of black card and covering them in fur fabric or scrunched-up tissue paper. Fasten on pipe-cleaner legs and add eyes. Display the web and the spiders on the wall.

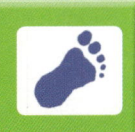

Stepping Stone
Value and contribute to own well-being and self-control.

Early Learning Goal
Work as part of a group or class, taking turns and sharing fairly, understanding that there needs to be agreed values and codes of behaviour for groups of people, including adults and children, to work together harmoniously.

Support and extension
Help younger children weave the wool through the web by pushing up the wool from underneath for the children to 'catch' and push back down the next hole, into the adult's hand. Invite pairs of older children to make their own miniature webs with a marble on a circle of black paper in a tub. When dry draw on the rings with a glue pen and sprinkle with glitter.

Home partnership
Ask parents and carers to look for webs around the home and garden and in books.

Further ideas
♦ Go for a walk together and search for spider's webs.
♦ Draw webs with silver pens on black paper, inviting the children to take turns to add lines.

Harvest celebrations

Group size
Whole group.

What you need
Adult dressed as a scarecrow; sack containing pictures of harvesting crops and harvest celebrations around the world (try international charities and the internet); box containing foods harvested locally such as fruit, vegetables, grains; basket of different types of bread, including those from different cultures.

Preparation
Ask for parents' permission to taste foods and check for any allergies and dietary requirements.

What to do
Explain to the children that a very special person who normally lives in a field has come to visit. Introduce the scarecrow and invite the children to ask him or her questions about his or her 'job'. Emphasise the important work farmers do and the jobs the scarecrow sees the farmers carrying out to ensure that there are lots of crops to harvest. Talk about harvest being a time for saying 'thank you' for all the good things we have in our lives, food being just one of them. Explore the contents of the food box together.

Ask the scarecrow to show the children what is in the sack and look at the pictures of harvest celebrations around the world together. Explain that many people take part in celebrations to think about how nature, and the work of farmers, helps provide our food. Encourage the children to tell the scarecrow about what they see and do at harvest time, such as what they see growing or being harvested locally, for sale in the shops, decorating places of worship and special celebrations.

Talk about harvest being a time for sharing and caring and how many people give food to those in need. Tell the children that the scarecrow has brought something to share with them. Look at different types of breads in the basket and share them out so everyone can taste the different types.

Support and extension
Split the activity into two or three separate sessions for younger children. Provide materials for older children to paint or make a harvest-time picture.

Home partnership
Ask parents and carers if they can donate food for boxes to give to local charities.

Further ideas
♦ Make bread to give to a special person.
♦ Collect food and place in decorated boxes to give to a local charity helping people in need.
♦ Listen to a recording of 'Harvest for the World' by The Isley Brothers (Sony/Legacy) or a similar song.

Theme links
Food
Our community

Foundation
Themes
Seasons

Time for bed

Stepping Stone
Demonstrate a sense of pride in own achievement.

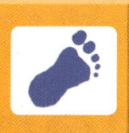

Early Learning Goal
Dress and undress independently and manage their own personal hygiene.

Group size
Small groups.

What you need
Bedtime story such as *Can't you sleep Little Bear?* by Martin Waddell (Walker Books); bedroom role-play area: torches, pillows, quilts, soft toys with night clothes, pyjamas, slippers, dressing gowns with assorted fastenings, lullaby CDs or tapes and player, books about bedtime and night, alarm clock.

What to do
Read a bedtime story to the children and encourage them to share their experiences about bedtime, both the good things and any fears they might have, such as the dark. Talk about how it starts to become dark earlier during autumn, and that it is soon going to be dark when they go to bed and get up in the morning. Help the children to think of fun things that they like to do in the dark, such as listening to a story by torch light, listening to music or having tea in their pyjamas.

Introduce the children to the bedroom role-play area and encourage them to explore it and the available resources. Invite them to get ready for bed by putting the pyjamas, slippers and dressing gowns on, encouraging them to try to do them up themselves and praising their efforts. Enact bedtime, brushing teeth, reading each other a story, climbing into bed and asking for drinks or a cuddly toy.

Set the alarm to go off at the end of the play session and encourage the children to take off the night clothes and put on their clothes and shoes.

Support and extension
Provide soft toys with night clothes for younger children who do not want to dress up themselves. Play getting ready for bed games with older children, rolling a dice where 6 means take off shoes, 5 put on a dressing gown and so on.

Home partnership
Ask parents and carers to help resource the role-play area. Invite them to send in a favourite bedtime story. Encourage parents to develop a structured bedtime at home with stories and cuddly toys.

Further ideas
♦ Sort out clothing by the types of fastenings they have and try on the clothes.
♦ Have a clothes shop role-play area.
♦ Give children 'I can' certificates when they can manage different fastenings.

Theme links
Our day
Stories and rhymes

The little red hen

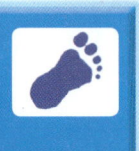
Group size
Whole group; small groups.

What you need
Big book or enlarged copy of 'The Little Red Hen' story (Traditional); hen glove puppet; simple outline drawings of the characters in the story made into stick puppets; card shapes; glue; scissors; drawing materials; thin dowel or plant sticks; adhesive tape; blank big book; marker pens.

What to do
Remind the children about the work that farmers do in autumn when they cut down the crops at harvest time. Introduce the hen puppet, explaining that she is going to tell the children the story of what happened to a friend of hers who lived on a farm whose name was The Little Red Hen. As the hen puppet reads the story to the children encourage them to use the pictures for clues as to what might be happening and who the characters are in the story. Invite them to predict the text and 'read' with you the repeating phrases.

Introduce the stick puppets for the main characters. Use these, together with pictures from the book, to help the children re-tell the story.

Working in groups, invite the children to make stick puppets by drawing pictures of the characters on to separate card shapes and securing them to a stick with tape. Encourage the children to use the puppets to make up their own stories of the Little Red Hen, scribing the stories for them into the blank big book, one on each double-page spread. Ask the children to illustrate their stories. Help the children to read the stories back to the hen glove puppet.

Support and extension
Provide outline drawings on card for younger children to decorate and make into puppets. Help older children write the name of the character on to the card puppet.

Home partnership
Send home a simple copy of the story for parents to share with their children. Invite them to make it into a book by helping their children to add a decorated front and back cover.

Further ideas
♦ Ask children to sequence a set of pictures and re-tell the story.
♦ Record the children's stories on to tape to use with the class big book.
♦ Re-read the story in the spring and plant wheat using the text to remind children how to look after it.

Theme links
Farms
Food
Traditional tales

Foundation
Themes
Seasons

Apple and spice garlands

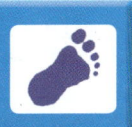

Group size
Small groups.

What you need
A3 sheet of paper; mixing bowl; tablespoons; teaspoon; wooden spoon; flour; apple puree; cinnamon or mixed spice; oven or microwave; leaves; table knives; cutters in shapes such as leaves, apples, trees, acorns or hedgehogs; rolling pins; drinking straw; PVA glue; green, brown, yellow, orange paint; brushes; thin ribbon in autumn colours; tree branches.

Preparation
On the A3 sheet of paper draw up a list of ingredients and equipment and simple instructions to make spiced apple dough.

What to do
Explain to the children that they are going to make an autumn garland that smells like autumn apple pies.
With the children read and follow the instructions to make the spiced apple dough. Invite them to roll out the dough and make autumn shapes using the cutters or by cutting around a small leaf with a knife.

Show the children how to make a hole at the top and bottom of each shape with a straw so that a ribbon can be threaded through. Bake the shapes slowly in a low oven or on defrost in the microwave until dry. When dry, varnish with PVA glue tinted with paint if desired. Help the children to thread their shapes on to lengths of ribbon to make garlands and secure these to branches with some hanging down and some in loops. Enjoy the aroma of spice and apples from the shapes.

Support and extension
Give hand-over-hand support as appropriate when younger children are mixing, rolling or cutting out their shapes. Make a game for older children to play, matching pictures of how to make the garlands to words (such as mix, roll, bake) or simple sentences if appropriate.

Home partnership
Send home an autumn dough shape on a ribbon for parents and carers to hang up and fragrance a room.

Further ideas
◆ Take photographs at each stage of making the garlands. Mount these in a book or on card and ask the children to describe what is happening in each one. Scribe their words below each photograph and display them near to the finished garlands.

> **Spiced apple dough**
> 3 tablespoons plain flour
> 1 tablespoon cinnamon or mixed spice
> apple puree
> ◆ Place flour and cinnamon or mixed spice in a bowl.
> ◆ Add apple puree, a teaspoonful at a time and mix until a soft, but not sticky, dough is made. It should be like play dough so the children can roll it out easily.

Theme links
Fruit
Our senses

Leaf litter confetti

Group size
Small groups.

What you need
Unlabelled autumn displays; marker pen; A3 paper; card; scissors; pencil; glue pen; dry colourful leaves; plastic containers.

Preparation
Make some sample labels using the 'leaf litter confetti'.

What to do
With each group of children look at an autumn display and talk about what they can see. Record their ideas on the A3 sheet of paper. Encourage the children to think of single words and simple phrases to describe what they can see. Explain that they are going to use these words to make labels for the display using a glue pen and special 'leaf litter confetti'. Show the children the sample labels and invite them to trace over the letters with their fingers.

Together, make the 'confetti' by crumbling the dry leaves into tiny pieces and placing it in the plastic containers. Invite each child to choose a word or phrase they would like to make for the display, such as 'crunchy leaves' or 'brown and orange'. Ask them to suggest a shape for the piece of card on which the word or phrase will be written, such as a leaf shape, a circle or a rectangle. Draw the outline on the card and invite the child to cut it out and then write the word or phrase on to the label in pencil for them.

Show the children how to trace over each letter, one at a time, with the glue pen and to sprinkle it with the leaf confetti while the glue is still wet. Leave the labels to dry before mounting them. Invite the children to place them on the display.

Support and extension
Give hand-over-hand support while younger children are using the glue pen. Have a selection of pre-cut shapes from which they can choose. Encourage older children to write their own words on to the card.

Home partnership
Suggest that parents and carers take their children on a walk to collect leaves and twigs to make confetti at home.

Further ideas
♦ Using the leaf confetti make leaf-shaped name cards. Ask the children to place them on an outline of a tree when they arrive at the setting and under the tree when they leave.
♦ Invite the children to form the letters on the display labels using whole tiny leaves.

Theme links
Natural materials
Plants

Apple tree bingo

Group size
Six children.

What you need
Card; Blu-Tack; laminating materials; the photocopiable sheet 'Apple tree bingo' on page 93; nine red or green counters for each child; numerals 1 to 9; bag; apple stickers.

Preparation
To prepare the boards make one copy of the photocopiable page on card and one on paper. To make other boards cut up the paper copy and rearrange the trees on to a piece of card. Hold them in place with Blu-Tack and make a card copy. Rearrange again to make a different board. When you have a total of six different boards laminate them all. Make one more card copy and cut it up into separate trees.

Theme links
Fruit
Number games

What to do
Talk about how we harvest apples from the trees in the autumn. Show the children the separate apple tree cards and numbers in the bag. Take the numbers out of the bag one at a time and encourage the children to say what each one is and to find the matching apple tree card, placing the number on the card. Next shuffle the tree cards and turn them over, one at a time, inviting the children to find the corresponding number and drop it in the bag.

Give out the boards and counters and explain to the children that they are going to play apple tree bingo, placing a counter on the tree on their board that matches the number pulled out of the bag. Play the game through, encouraging the children to shout 'bingo' when all the trees are matched. Reward their careful counting with an apple sticker each.

Support and extension
Prepare boards to suit the needs of younger children by selecting the appropriate apple trees on the photocopiable page (such as 1 to 3) and placing them in a row to copy on to card. Play the first bingo game. For more confident or older children, play 'Bingo threes', with a winner. Invite the children to shout 'bingo' when they get three trees in a row across or down.

Home partnership
Invite parents and carers to borrow the gameboards to play at home with their children.

Further ideas
♦ Make a set of tree cards to match to a board showing numbers only.
♦ Cut open apples and count the seeds. Make a corresponding paper number and glue the seeds on to the number.
♦ Roll a number dice, find the matching number sticker and place it on a piece of paper and make a corresponding set of apple prints next to it.

Squirrel hide-and-seek

Stepping Stone
Find items from positional/directional clues.
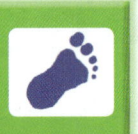

Early Learning Goal
Use everyday words to describe position.

Group size
Six children.

What you need
Small toy squirrel; small-world trees and bushes, or trimmings from real ones mounted in steady bases; dry leaves; small plastic plant pots; Cellophane puddles; small logs; copy of the song 'Where is squirrel?' on the photocopiable sheet on page 84.

What to do
Talk about how squirrels can be seen in the autumn, eating berries and nuts from the trees. Show the children the resources and ask them to help you to arrange them on a table ready to play a game. While the children are occupied, hide the squirrel inside one of the plant pots before putting it on the floor last of all. Tell the children that a little squirrel is playing hide and seek and invite a child in turn to try and find it. Repeat the game, hiding the squirrel while the children turn around, until every child has had a turn. Encourage the use of positional language to describe where the squirrel was found such as inside the pots, underneath the leaves or between the trees.

Explain to the children that the squirrel has a special song for them to learn. Introduce the song and then invite the children to sing it with you taking turns to place the squirrel in the correct place as each verse is sung. Encourage them to make up new verses to use as they play the games with their friends.

Support and extension
With young children introduce the positions gradually reinforcing the new position each time, for example 'under' the leaves, the pot, the bush. Change the song verses to reinforce this position. Extend the activity for older children by putting squirrels on, under, behind, in front and between plant pots. Ask the children to close their eyes while you remove a squirrel. Can they describe which one is missing?

Home partnership
Encourage parents and carers to play games such as 'Hunt the Teddy' with their children, hiding a soft toy and giving clues to its position, for example 'He's inside something' or 'He's up high'.

Further ideas
♦ Arrange the resources as a woodland walk. Ask the children to describe a walk for the squirrel to take and invite another child to help the squirrel to follow it.
♦ Hide pictures of squirrels around the setting and ask one child to find it. They must then explain its position to a friend who tries to find it. This child explains where it was to another child, to hide again and so on.

Theme links
Animals
Toy and games

The apple challenge

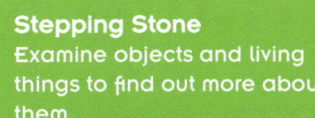

Stepping Stone
Examine objects and living things to find out more about them.

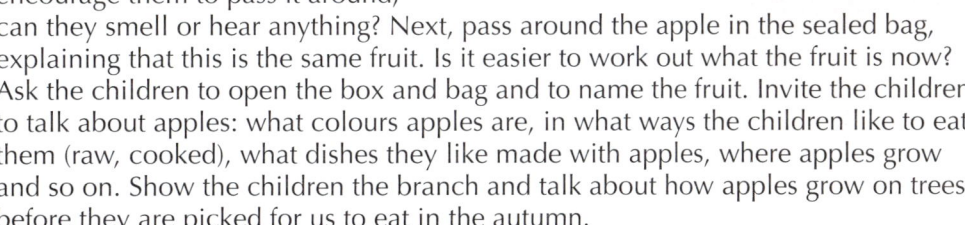

Early Learning Goal
Investigate objects and materials by using all of their senses as appropriate.

Group size
Small groups.

What you need
Two apples; box; bag; other apples and edible apple-based products such as varieties of fresh apples, tinned, compote, purée, chutney, pies, fruit bars, biscuits; apple scented products such as bubble bath, shampoo, candles, food magazines; recipe leaflets; paper; paints; drawing materials; small branch from an apple tree, with apples on it; copy of the song 'Apple song' on the photocopiable sheet on page 88.

Preparation
Place an apple in a sealed box and another in a bag. Ask for parents' permission to taste foods and check for any allergies and dietary requirements.

What to do
Invite the children to guess what fruit is inside the sealed box, encourage them to pass it around, can they smell or hear anything? Next, pass around the apple in the sealed bag, explaining that this is the same fruit. Is it easier to work out what the fruit is now? Ask the children to open the box and bag and to name the fruit. Invite the children to talk about apples: what colours apples are, in what ways the children like to eat them (raw, cooked), what dishes they like made with apples, where apples grow and so on. Show the children the branch and talk about how apples grow on trees before they are picked for us to eat in the autumn.

Set up taste tables where the children can try the different apples and apple products. Place the apple scented products on a separate table and invite the children to smell them. In another area set up printing and drawing activities for the children to record what they see, both with whole apples and cut apples.

Display the collection of apples and apple-based products, the children's drawings, printing activities and an apple-shaped collage of pictures the children find in magazines and on labels from packaging showing apple products.

Support and extension
Give adult support to younger children for the table-based activities. Make individual booklets with older children showing apple prints, observational drawings and apple products cut from magazine pictures.

Home partnership
Ask parents and carers to send in apple-based items for the displays.

Further ideas
◆ Learn the 'Apple song' on the photocopiable sheet.
◆ Find simple recipes using apples and make some of them.
◆ List all the ways of using apples that the children can find on the trunk of a paper apple tree. Add this to the display.
◆ Plant apple seeds and watch them grow.

Theme links
Food
Fruit

Catch the wind

Stepping Stone
Talk about what is seen and what is happening.

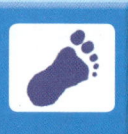

Early Learning Goal
Look closely at similarities, differences, patterns and change.

Group size
Whole group.

What you need
A windy day; crêpe-paper streamers; ribbons; carrier bags; commercially-made windmills; copy of *The Wind Blew* by Pat Hutchins (Red Fox); two large blankets; bubbles; two pieces of dowel; bin bag; sticky tape; string.

What to do
Invite the children to wrap up warmly and go outside on a windy day. Encourage them to run into and away from the wind, to feel it on their hair, their faces and their clothes. Ask them to stop and stand still and watch what happens to trees, leaves, birds, clouds and other things in the immediate environment. Can they describe what is happening and how the things are moving? Ask them why they think this is happening and how would the things move if the wind was stronger, like a gale, or more gentle, like a breeze. Invite the children to try and catch any leaves or pieces of paper blowing around and to run with streamers, ribbons and windmills watching the effect the wind has on them. Suggest they run with carrier bags and catch the wind. (Emphasise the safe use of these bags).

Spread a blanket on the ground and invite the children to sit down for a story, placing the other blanket over them. Read *The Wind Blew*, while sitting outside and compare the story to the things they experienced.

Support and extension
Work in small groups with adult support to ensure that younger children fully experience feeling the effect of the wind. With older children show them how to make a wind line by tying ribbons, crêpe paper streamers, clothes, threaded milk bottle tops and small metal objects to a washing line and to watch them move in the wind.

Home partnership
Suggest parents and carers go for a walk with their children so they can experience the wind in different places, such as at the beach, in a park or the shopping area.

Further ideas
♦ Blow bubbles and let a bag of leaves go and compare how they move in the wind. Can the children catch any of them?
♦ Make kites from two crossed pieces of dowel secured with sticky tape, backed with a diamond-shaped piece of bin bag. Add a crêpe paper tail and string. Encourage the children to try out and modify their designs.

Theme links
Stories
Weather

Tree treasure boxes

Stepping Stone
Begin to try out a range of tools and techniques safely.

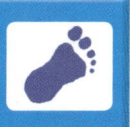

Early Learning Goal
Select the tools and techniques they need to shape, assemble and join materials they are using.

Group size
Small groups.

What you need
The photocopiable sheet 'Treasure boxes' on page 94 copied on to card for each child; scissors; glue sticks; paper; wax crayons; paint; twigs; small leaves; safe outdoor area with trees; paper bags.

What to do

Go for a walk with the children and talk about the trees around them. Invite children to go on a tree treasure hunt looking for leaves, twigs, seeds and pieces of bark they find on the ground. Give each child a paper bag to hold their treasures. Encourage them to touch the bark on different trees, feeling the different textures, and to find one they like. Show the children how to take a bark rubbing in pairs, with one child holding the paper against the trunk while the other rubs the flat side of a wax crayon over the paper. Place the rubbing in the paper bag.

Back inside, show the children a card copy of the tree box and explain that this is a tree treasure box in which to place their treasures from the walk. Demonstrate how to cut out, fold and glue the tree box. Help the children to make their boxes and then decorate them by painting the tree before placing a piece of the bark rubbing on the trunk and adding leaves and twigs to the top. Invite the children to select their favourite things from the walk to place inside the boxes.

Support and extension

Provide younger children with pre-cut boxes. Give older children glue, sticky tape and staplers to secure the boxes. Invite them to compare the finished results, before choosing how to make their final box.

Home partnership

Invite parents and carers to help their child make a string of paper trees from a long strip of folded paper and to decorate them with natural materials that they have found on a walk.

Further ideas

♦ Help the children make feely boxes or bags containing items from a tree such as bark pieces, twigs, leaves, pine cones for others to explore.
♦ Invite children to make collages by cutting out leaf or tree shapes from paper and fastening on natural materials collected on the walk.

Theme links
Materials
Trees

Hedgehog art

Stepping Stone
Complete a simple program on the computer and/or perform simple functions on ICT apparatus.

Early Learning Goal
Find out about and identify the uses of everyday technology and use information and communication technology and programmable toys to support their learning.

Group size
Whole group, in pairs.

What you need
Computer with a simple paint program such as RM Colour Magic; colour printer; paper; wildlife video featuring hedgehogs and viewing facilities or internet access; photographs of hedgehogs.

Preparation
Carry out a search and find relevant web sites with information on hedgehogs. For example, try putting 'hedgehog preservation' in a search engine and make a note of those suitable to use with the group. Print out care instructions to send home.

What to do
Together with the children watch a video on hedgehogs or visit a relevant web site and look at the shape, colour and features of a hedgehog. Talk about how hedgehogs prepare for winter, when food is short, by making a nest of leaves in which to hibernate. Look at the photographs and draw the children's attention to the shape of the hedgehog's face and body and the spikes on its back.

Demonstrate how to use the paint program on the computer, showing the children how to change the colours and use the brush, pencil and undo/redo facility. Invite the children to use the computer in pairs to draw a simple hedgehog. Encourage them to change their designs if they are not happy with them and to print out their final versions.

Mount the hedgehog pictures low down along a wall. Ask the children to glue leaves on to paper to make a nest for each hedgehog and use these as lift-up flaps to hide the sleeping hedgehogs.

Support and extension
Help younger children to make a hedgehog shape by drawing a simple outline on to tracing paper and securing it to the monitor screen with low tack putty. Help them follow the outline to draw their hedgehog using the mouse. Encourage older children to use the internet to find a photograph of a hedgehog to print out. Help them to enter a website address such as www.freefoto.com select the picture and use the print icon.

Home partnership
Send home a copy of the children's hedgehog pictures together with simple care instructions printed out from a website, detailing what to feed hedgehogs, why not to use slug pellets, how to provide hibernation places and what to do if one is found in your garden.

Further ideas
♦ Save the children's artwork to a file and use to create a computer slide show the children can watch.
♦ Listen to a taped story about hedgehogs such as *The Hodgeheg* by Dick King-Smith (BBC Audio).

Theme links
Animals
Gardens
Preparing for winter

Making a corn dolly

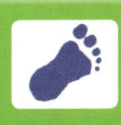

Stepping Stone
Manipulate materials to achieve a planned effect.

Early Learning Goal
Handle tools, objects, construction and malleable materials safely and with increasing control.

What to do

Sit in a circle and pass the corn dollies and photographs around for the children to examine carefully. Explain that a very long time ago the Romans and Celts used to honour the spirit of the corn and other gods of nature at harvest time, to say 'thank you' for the crops and food. They made corn dollies, or corn mothers, from the last sheaf of wheat to be cut and kept it safe until next harvest. After bringing home this last sheaf there was a feast and dancing. Help the children look at the corn dollies more closely, describing the twisted designs or tied bundles and looking at the seed heads.

Invite the children to make a simple corn dolly by binding bundles of corn stalks or art straws together with thin thread near the top. Show them how to tie it again to form a neck and splay out the top like hair, then split the bundle in two half-way down to form legs. Next, secure with thread at the start and end of each leg and weave straws through the body to make the arms. Attach a thread to the top of each dolly and display them against a dark background along with the harvest pictures and photographs and the examples of corn dollies.

Support and extension

As a simpler alternative, draw a corn dolly outline on to paper and invite younger children to glue on straws filling in the shape. Encourage older children to draw their corn dolly on to black paper with a gold pen.

Home partnership

Ask parents to bring in examples of items made from corn, wheat or straw to show the children.

Further ideas

♦ Invite children to design corn dollies in heart or cone shapes. Encourage them to twist, weave or plait the straws.
♦ Make bread dough, following a simple recipe or using a packet mix. Form into the shape of a sheaf of wheat and ask each child to make a stalk to add to the sheaf. Use clean scissors or a knife to cut snips for the ears.

Theme links
Food
Harvest
Traditional crafts

Making an autumn picnic

Stepping Stone
Show awareness of a range of healthy practices with regard to eating, sleeping and hygiene.

Early Learning Goal
Recognise the importance of keeping healthy and those things which contribute to this.

Group size
Whole group.

What you need
Examples of food with an autumn theme, such as apples, pears, plums, potatoes, carrots, corn-on-the-cob; examples of foods made from these, such as apple or pear spread, plum jam, assorted vegetable crisps, bread and cornflakes; tablecloth; safe knives; chopping boards; plastic picnic boxes; blanket.

Preparation
Ask for parents' permission to taste foods and check for any allergies and dietary requirements.

What to do
Sit in a circle, set out the tablecloth and arrange the different unprocessed foods on it. Invite the children to name the foods they know as they are displayed. Talk about where they grow (on trees, under the ground or in a field) and how we harvest them in the autumn.

Introduce the remaining products and encourage the children to think which of the foods already on the cloth these products are made from. Talk about why these natural foods are good for us, and how we should eat only a little of them when they are turned into products such as jam or crisps, as these foods contain a lot of sugar or fat.

Invite the children to help make an autumn picnic to take with them on a walk. Explain that they must wash their hands before preparing food. Help the children to prepare simple, easily carried food such as chopped apples, plums and pears, some threaded on to cocktail sticks to make fruit kebabs, sandwiches, baby baked potatoes, carrot sticks with a dip and chocolate cornflake cakes. Pack the food in plastic boxes.

Go for a brisk autumn walk and sit on a blanket to enjoy the picnic food

Support and extension
Provide hand-over-hand support when younger children are cutting up fruit and vegetables. Ask older children to think of active games to play while on the walk.

Home partnership
Invite parents and carers to go on the picnic with you, reinforcing the idea of healthy eating by asking them to bring a healthy snack to share.

Further ideas
◆ Make a display of autumn fruit and vegetables and healthy products made from them, with samples to taste.
◆ Invite the children to make soup based on autumn vegetables.
◆ Visit a 'pick-your-own' farm and pick fruit and vegetables to use at the setting.

Theme links
Days out
Healthy eating
Seasonal food

An autumn journey stick

Stepping Stone
Try to capture experiences and responses with music, dance, paint and other materials or words.

Early Learning Goal
Respond in a variety of ways to what they see, hear, smell, touch and feel.

Group size
Whole group.

What you need
Strong branch or stick, about 60cm long; raffia; natural items collected on an autumn walk; paper; writing materials; glue gun.

What to do
Explain to the children that they are going for a walk to collect some natural items. They are then going to use the leaves, twigs, seeds, dried grasses and feathers they have collected to make a record of their walk by making a journey stick.

Take the children on a walk through the local countryside, a park, woods or nature reserve and encourage them to collect one or two very special fallen items each, such as a beautiful leaf, feather or small piece of bark. While on the walk encourage the children to use their senses, stopping and listening to the sounds around them, comparing the size and shape of the trees, touching the bark, smelling the air and the scent of trees and damp leaves.

Back in the setting work with small groups of children at a time, to make up the journey stick. Invite them to talk about their special items to the other children in their group. Show them how to fasten the collected items to the branch by binding on each item with raffia.

Encourage the children to make small drawings of the walk and to add these to the stick together with their name.

When the stick is complete, pass it around in small groups to help the children remember the walk and what they experienced.

Support and extension
With younger children secure the item in place with a cold melt glue gun before helping them tie the raffia. Encourage older children to make their own sticks while they are on the walk, working in a group of three or four, and binding on an item each time they stop and pick one up.

Home partnership
Encourage families to make a journey stick of their own, based on a recent walk. Invite them to bring these into the setting to share with others and ask them to describe their walks.

Further ideas
♦ Use the stick as a stimulus for writing a simple poem to describe the walk.
♦ Make a stick to record a day in the setting, starting at the bottom and adding items as the day progresses.

Theme links
Journeys
Outdoor environment

Foundation Themes
Seasons

Autumn art

Early Learning Goal
Explore colour, texture, shape, form and space in two or three dimensions.

Group size
Individuals.

What you need
Pictures showing autumnal scenes, such as *Herald of Autumn* by Paul Klee or *Autumn leaves* by Georgia O'Keeffe; paint, pastels and paper in neutral and autumnal shades; brushes; scissors; glue.

What to do
Display the pictures for the children to look at and talk together about why they make us think of autumn.
Develop the idea of how the artist selects colours to emphasise the environment and the things within it. Think about the colours of autumn being more muted and softer in colour than summer, when the sun is bright. Find the focal points in the pictures, such as a beautiful leaf or tree in autumn colours. Encourage the children to think of other things associated with autumn that could make a focal point, such as a conker in its shell, acorns or a spray of berries.

Invite the children to paint their own autumn pictures. Help them select a colour and size of paper and paint a background to reflect an autumn day, perhaps in the sun or mist, out in the woods and a pile of leaves. Encourage them to experiment with mixing paint to make the shades they want. When dry add the focal point to the picture. Help the children cut paper to shape and then add detail with pastels. Encourage children to think about where to place this symbol to enhance the picture, before gluing in place.

Ask the children to sign their picture and think of a title. Display the children's work with the original pictures and the autumn artefacts.

Support and extension
Support younger children by providing just two or three colours of paint which mix well together. Provide templates or pre-cut shapes for the focal point. Cut strips of paper and encourage older children to make frames, decorating them with leaf prints or bark rubbings.

Home partnership
Invite parents and carers in to view the finished display. Suggest they look out for signs of autumn with their children as they walk to and from your setting.

Further ideas
◆ Let the children make pictures with a mixture of painted backgrounds and autumn items as 3-D collages.
◆ Weave strips of paper in autumn colours through a painted leaf or tree shape.

Theme links
Colour
Famous artists

Chapter 4

Winter

Develop the children's skills across the whole curriculum with these ideas for cold, dark winter days. Find out how fires and candlelight help us through this season and how animals deal with the harsh winter weather with the variety of activities contained within this chapter.

Feed the birds

What you need / Group size / Preparation sidebar

Theme links
Nature
Our environment

What to do

Gather all the children and look at the pictures of the birds together, naming the different kinds. Talk about how birds can have difficulty finding enough food and water to stay alive during the winter. Ask if the children know why, before explaining that in cold weather there are very few insects, seeds or berries to eat and that water freezes, so birds have nothing to eat, drink or bathe in. Invite the children to start a bird feeding area providing high energy bird cake, food and water.

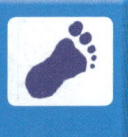

Stepping Stone
Show care and concern for others, for living things and the environment.

Early Learning Goal
Consider the consequences of their words and actions for themselves and others.

In small groups make the bird cake by melting the fat then allowing it to cool. Place a long length of string in the yoghurt pot, curling some into the bottom, the rest draped over the side to hang it up. Pour the fat in to the pot until half full, then invite the children to stir in some seeds, nuts, biscuits and fruit. Leave to set before tipping out.

Take groups of children outside to hang up their bird cake from the tree or washing line. Place a saucer of water and scatter some food and bird cake on the bird table.

Make a feeding rota of groups of children to replenish the food and water. Emphasise the importance of remembering to do this as the birds become reliant on the food for survival.

Support and extension

With younger children mix the bird cake in a bigger bowl, then spoon into yoghurt pots. Encourage older children to make a bird table from a flat piece of wood with a ledge added to the sides. Secure in the ground or hang from a tree.

Home partnership

Invite parents and carers in on a daily rota basis to help the groups feed the birds.

Further ideas

♦ Help the children to identify the birds they see and contact the Royal Society for the Protection of Birds at www.rspb.org for information about helping birds.

Winter market

Group size
Small groups.

What you need
Tables; paper; card; glitter; paint in pots; sponges; fabric pieces; pot pourri; small bags; ribbons; candles; fir cones; pieces of evergreen plants; oasis in a pot; cloves; oranges; shopping bags; till; money; fairy lights; CD of winter music and CD player; winter coats; hats; gloves; table; glue; scissors; crayons.

Preparation
Set up a role-play winter market with stalls in one area displaying items to buy. Change the range of items regularly to ensure interest and motivation remain high and different gifts can be made. Set the scene with the lights and music. Place the clothing and table for making gifts nearby.

What to do
Explain to the children that many towns and cities hold special winter markets where people go to buy gifts, or items from which to make gifts. Show them the role-play area and switch on the lights and play the music. Invite them to look at the items displayed and encourage them to use their imagination to think of gifts that they could make. These could include:
♦ a card in wintry colours
♦ sponge-printed gift wrap and tag
♦ hanging decorations
♦ pot pourri and fir cones in bags, tied with ribbon
♦ clove studded oranges
♦ candles and evergreen arranged in oasis.
    Invite the children to visit the market, dressing in winter clothes to buy items they need to make a gift of their choice. Encourage them to take turns to be the customer and market trader before moving to the craft area to make their gift. Model techniques to make the items as required.

Support and extension
For younger children provide some examples of gifts and cards to make, which can be easily copied and provide adult support. Encourage older children to price the goods for sale and pay for the items selected.

Home partnership
Send home information on the winter market and invite parents and carers to order a gift from their child.

Further ideas
♦ 'Buy' ingredients to make simple sweets such as chocolate-dipped fruit or balls of crushed biscuits, fruit and melted chocolate.
♦ Visit a market and choose something special for the setting, such as a plant or cushion.
♦ Make posters for the market stalls.

Theme links
Gifts and giving
Shopping

Winter rap

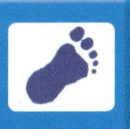
Group size
Groups of eight children.

What you need
Large box; silver paper; winter pictures and items such as trees, landscapes, ice, snow, holly, clothing, snowflakes, evergreen plants, snowmen, blazing fires, presents, candles; A3 paper; marker pen; silver marker pen; blue paper strips; percussion instruments.

Preparation
Wrap the box in silver paper and place the winter pictures and items inside it.

What to do
Sit the children in a horseshoe shape so they can see both the box and paper. Ask the children to share ideas on what winter means to them. Explain that in the box are some things associated with winter. Pass the box around the group and ask the children to take turns to pull an item or picture out. Ask the children to listen while an adult says the word clearly, emphasising the initial and end sounds. Invite the children to repeat the word and name first the initial sound and then the end one. Ask if they can hear any sounds in the middle of the word. Model writing the word, naming the sounds.

Ask four or five children to select an item each. Encourage all the children to think of words with same initial sounds to make a pair or phrase such as 'dark days', 'flaming fires', 'slippery, slushy snow'. Model writing these phrases on to separate strips of blue paper using silver marker pen and large lettering. Say the phrases to the children emphasising the alliteration.

Encourage them to place the phrases into a sequence to make a rap. Clap out the rhythm of the rap, one clap to each syllable. Repeat the rap, introducing musical instruments to emphasise the rhythm.

Support and extension
Support younger children by saying three phrases and asking them to listen for the one with the same initial sounds, 'brown trees, winter trees, tall trees'.
Ask older children to write over the initial sounds of the words in silver glitter-glue.

Home partnership
Suggest families make up a short rap for a favourite item in the home.

Further ideas
♦ Think of words that rhyme with items in the box, such as 'nice ice', 'bright light'.
♦ Hide pictures of winter items or the item themselves in real or fake snow and sort them by initial sounds.

Theme links
Music
Sounds

Foundation Themes
Seasons

Candlelight poetry

Stepping Stone
Build up vocabulary that reflects the breadth of their experiences.

Early Learning Goal
Extend their vocabulary, exploring the meanings and sounds of new words.

Group size
Groups of eight children.

What you need
Assorted candles; tray of sand; small candle for each child; tea lights; matches; low table; writing materials; paper; extra adult.

What to do

Arrange the tray of candles on the low table and position the children around it in a semicircle, a safe distance away. Talk about why candle light is beautiful on dark winter nights. Pass around the small candles and feel the wax and wick. Emphasise candle safety, then carefully light the candles. Watch them burn and talk about what the children can see. Encourage them to think of words to describe the candle burning. Introduce new vocabulary such as 'flame', 'melting', 'dripping', 'trickling',' flickering' and 'glimmering'. List these words and any others that the children can think of on a sheet of paper.

Use the suggested words to make a simple five-line poem using a starting-point for each line, such as line 1 – shape and size, line 2 – colour, line 3 – the flame, and so on. Scribe or ask the children to copy the finished poems on to candle outlines and display these together with the (unlit) candles.

Support and extension

Encourage younger children to take part in the first part of the activity, writing the descriptive words on candle shapes to display around a large painted candle. Help older children write an acrostic poem, writing the word candle down a sheet of paper and thinking up a line starting with each letter to describe the candles.

Home partnership

Send copies of the poems written on a candle shape together with an explanation of the activity and candle safety information for children to talk about with their parents and carers at home.

Further ideas

♦ Decorate candle shapes with descriptive words written in wax crayon. Paint over with a colour wash.
♦ Invite children to bring in candles to display with the candle poems. Ask them to think of three words to describe it and place them alongside the candle.
♦ Play 'I spy', describing a candle for the children to find.

Theme links
Celebrations
Light and dark

Jolly snowmen

Stepping Stone
Show an interest in number problems.

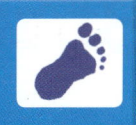

Early Learning Goal
In practical activities and discussion begin to use the vocabulary involved in adding and subtracting.

Group size
Six or eight children, then working in pairs

What you need
White toilet tissue, shredded; soap flakes; warm water; mixing bowl; electric whisk; copy of the rhyme 'Ten white snowmen' on the photocopiable sheet on page 85.

What to do
Gather the children together around a table and talk about what they enjoy about snowy days. Explain that they are going to make 'snow' which does not melt. Invite the children to place the shredded toilet tissue, soap flakes and warm water in the bowl and whisk them together to form a thick 'snow'.

Encourage each child to make a snowman from the mixture, then set number-based challenges for them. For example, 'make one bigger and one smaller one', 'make one more than Thomas', 'how many have to 'melt' to leave three?'.

Introduce the snowmen rhyme to the children. Ask them if they have enough snowmen between them to sing the rhyme through, or if they need to make more. Sing the rhyme through, removing a snowman each verse until none are left.

Encourage the children to work in pairs making enough snowmen to sing the rhyme through, taking turns to remove the snowmen as they count down.

Support and extension
For younger children base the activity on just five snowmen. With confident children introduce the idea of counting down in two's, with two snowmen melting each time.

Home partnership
Let the children take home copies of the rhyme to share and enjoy with their parents and carers.

Further ideas
♦ Hide snowmen under a white cloth. Remove some and place them on top. Ask the children how many snowmen are left.
♦ Use ready-to-roll icing to make a set of snowmen. Roll a dice and add currant buttons to match the number shown.
♦ Paint pictures of snowmen in white paint mixed with salt. Laminate them. Use for counting activities.

Theme links
Counting rhymes
Winter weather

Foundation Themes
Seasons

Blazing fires

Group size
Six or eight children working in pairs.

What you need
Sponges cut into shapes; red, orange, light brown and yellow paint in trays; black paper; pictures of bonfires and fires in fireplaces.

What to do
Talk to the children about the times they have seen blazing fires, such as outside for special winter celebrations on Bonfire night or at New Year, or to burn garden rubbish, and inside the home in fireplaces to warm us up on cold winter days. Ask the children to describe the colours and shapes they have seen in fires and compare their ideas with the fires in the pictures.

Show the children the printing materials and invite them to make fire pictures printing with the shape sponges. They could choose an outside bonfire, made with large sponge shapes for the flames and then small ones for the sparks or an inside fire with a fireplace of printed squares around the flames. Encourage the children to work a pattern into the flames, for example red triangle, orange diamond or large red square, small yellow circle.

Ask the children to print repeating patterns in fire colours on to strips of paper and use these to border a display of the fire pictures.

Support and extension
Invite younger children to continue a given pattern of printing shapes in one size and two colours. Extend the activity for older children by asking them to cut out bright fire-coloured card shapes with a slot in each. Show them how to slot these together to build a 3-D bonfire, with repeating patterns for the flames.

Home partnership
Compile a fire safety leaflet with the children and decorate it with a small printed bonfire using sponge shapes. Send copies home for parents and carers to discuss with their children.

Further ideas
♦ Draw shapes with a glue pen to represent the sparks and sprinkle with glitter.
♦ Cut out flames from paper and decorate with printed shapes. Display tucked into small logs, like a fire.
♦ Use recyclable materials to build models of bonfires.

Theme links
Colours
Hot and cold
Our homes

Hibernation holes

Stepping Stone
Describe simple features of objects and events.

Early Learning Goal
Find out about, and identify, some features of living things, objects and events they observe.

Group size
Eight to ten children.

What you need
Salt dough; paints; brushes; small pots; boxes; tubes; dried leaves; grass; plant compost; display area with table; books about hibernation; small plastic bats, snakes, frogs, hedgehogs, tortoise; small blanket.

Preparation
Place the blanket on the floor and place a mound of leaves and dry grass on top. Hide the plastic animals in the leaves.

What to do
Begin by sitting in a circle around the blanket. Talk about what we do in winter to keep warm, such as put on the heating and wear more clothes. Explain that animals and birds cannot do these things. Some, such as birds, stay alive by going to a warmer country and some eat more food in autumn to put on fat. Others get ready for winter in a special way, they hibernate, finding a warm, dry place and going into a very deep sleep until spring arrives.

Tell the children that under the leaves are examples of animals that hibernate for them to find. Use the books to find out where these animals hibernate.

Give each child a piece of salt dough and suggest that they make a model of a creature which hibernates, looking carefully at the plastic models and pictures to find its shape and features. Paint the models when they are dry. Encourage the children to select from the junk materials to make a place the right size for their creature and fill it with suitable bedding before placing the creature amongst it. They have made a hibernation hole. Display these together with pictures of the animals, books, the plastic models and bedding materials.

Support and extension
Let younger children make their creatures working in pairs, with adult support. Help older children use books to find out more about their chosen creatures.

Home partnership
Send home the 'hibernation holes' with a label saying 'Do not disturb until spring'. Keep them safe for a 'Wake up to spring' day.

Further ideas
♦ Paint a long mural showing how different animals cope in winter.
♦ Make a hibernating-animals book, hiding animal pictures under flaps, showing their hibernation place.
♦ Encourage hibernation role-play, with a den under a table.

Theme links
Animals
Homes

Once upon a winter's day

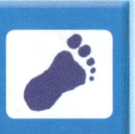
Group size
Whole group.

What you need
Picture of a typical winter scene; treasure box; white paper; selected prompts for talking about winter to include the weather, clothing, pictures and old cards with a winter scene, books, snow-shakers, model snowmen, sledges, fir trees; table; small boxes; white sheet; parents, grandparents and carers willing to share stories about winter.

Preparation
Wrap the treasure box in white paper and place the collected winter items inside. Cover the table with the white sheet, using the boxes to provide a range of levels.

Theme links
Families
In the past
Weather

What to do
For the first session, sit together near the table and look at the picture, asking questions about what the children can see and what time of year it might be. Talk about how winter is different to other seasons, especially the weather. Invite a child to come and take something out of the treasure box. Talk about why the item is associated with winter. Place the item on the table. Continue until all the items are on the table.

In subsequent sessions, invite an adult to bring in an item, photograph or picture related to winter and to share their winter experiences. Encourage the children to ask questions to find how they coped with the cold, wet, ice, fog and snow and what they enjoyed and did not enjoy doing in winter both when they were a child and as an adult.

Support and extension
For younger children place fewer items in the treasure box and break the activity down into a short daily session. For older children extend the activity by scribing the anecdotes into a book and inviting the children to paint and draw pictures to illustrate them.

Home partnership
Start a 'Winter memories' book, sending home a scrap book in which families record their memories of winter, through writing, poems and pictures.

Further ideas
♦ Ask a local newspaper to write about the work the setting is doing, inviting local people to send in their memories for inclusion in the 'Winter memories' book.
♦ Make a display of photos, pictures, books, children's artwork and clothing linked to winter. Place alongside the table.
♦ Make winter scenes from natural and recyclable materials for small-world play.

Evergreen plants

Group size
Whole group, with adult helpers.

What you need
Outdoor area with a variety of evergreen trees and bushes; small branches of holly, fir, ivy, pine, laurel; copy of the song 'Holly bushes lovely to see' on the photocopiable sheet on page 88; paper; drawing materials.

What to do
Familiarise yourself with the 'Holly bushes lovely to see' song. Wrap up in warm clothing and take a winter walk, looking closely at what happens to the plants and trees in winter. Encourage the children to spot those that still have their leaves and introduce the word 'evergreen'. As each plant is found sing the appropriate part of the song. Try to find leaves on the ground underneath trees that have lost theirs and take some back to the setting.

Back in the setting reinforce the plant names by singing the song through showing the children the appropriate branch that you have collected. Invite the children to carefully examine the evergreens and to compare the leaves with those they found on the ground. Encourage them to describe the leaves, using words such as 'thick, shiny, spiky holly' and 'thin, firm pine needles'. Explain that holly, laurel and ivy leaves are tougher and thicker than those on a plant that loses its leaves, the shiny surface stops water escaping and protects the leaf in winter. Talk about the pine needles being long and thin so there is less surface for water to escape than on a large flat leaf. Look at other features of the plants such as cones and berries, emphasising that some berries can be dangerous if eaten.

Encourage the children to make observational drawings of the evergreen plants and place these together in a book. Scribe the appropriate part of the song next to the drawings.

Support and extension
Invite younger children to sort the plants by the leaves they have, using criteria such as long and thin, flat, curved, spiky. Help older children to use a simple plant identification chart to find the names of the evergreen trees found on the walk.

Home partnership
Ask parents and carers to send in leaves from evergreen plants in their gardens.

Further ideas
♦ Press leaves into pieces of clay to make imprints.
♦ Photocopy different evergreen leaves to make silhouettes, then invite the children to match them to real leaves.

Theme links
Colour
Gardens
Trees and plants

Winter cave for a bear

Stepping Stone
Show an interest in ICT.

Early Learning Goal
Find out about and identify the uses of everyday technology and use information and communication technology and programmable toys to support their learning.

Group size
Small groups.

What you need
Programmable floor toy, such as Roamer; brown fur fabric; copy of the rhyme 'Sleepy, sleepy bear' on the photocopiable sheet on page 85; toy squirrel, frog, hedgehog, snake; tree-branches in a brown tube; blue cellophane stream; nest of grass; small rocks; chair or cardboard box cave; large floor area; blankets.

Preparation
Lay the animals and their homes, in the order that they are mentioned in the rhyme, at regular intervals along the floor in a straight line. Add brown fur fabric to the Roamer to look as though it is dressed as a bear.

What to do
Sit in a cosy area under blankets and talk about how cold it gets in winter. Introduce the bear Roamer to the children and ask them how they think he will keep warm in winter. Talk about how bears have fur that becomes thicker to insulate them from the cold and they sleep for long periods of time, in a dry place, such as a cave.

Share the rhyme with the children then show them the route based on it. Invite them to try to get the bear to his cave, stopping at each creature along the way. Show the children how to enter instructions into the Roamer and let them practice moving it until they are confident. Next, read one verse of the poem at a time while the children work out the moves to reach this animal, encouraging them to try again if necessary. When the bear reaches the cave tuck him in and say 'shhh sleep well!'

Support and extension
Support younger children by working out the moves together and recording them. Take turns to use these to program the Roamer while you read out the rhyme. Let older children put bears to sleep in box 'caves'. Use the computer to write a sign 'Shh! Bear in hibernation!' and decorate it with clip art pictures.

Home partnership
Make a story bag to send home containing a bear, a sturdy child's tape recorder and a story tape about a bear such as *Can't You Sleep Little Bear?* by Martin Waddell (Walker Books).

Further ideas
◆ Use websites such as www.sciencemadesimple.com/animals.html to find out more about hibernation.
◆ Read the story *When Will It Be Spring?* by Catherine Walters (Little Tiger Press) about a bear cub's first winter. Enact the story using the Roamer.

Theme links
Animals
Homes
Toys

Glitter, shine and sparkle

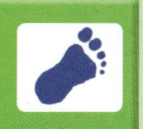
Group size
Small groups.

What you need
The photocopiable sheet 'Winter shapes' on page 95, copied on to card; scissors; PVA glue; shiny, glittery collage materials; glitter; sequins; wooden clothes pegs with the springs removed; cotton tips; white and silver paint; salt; silver thread; CD player and CD of winter music.

Preparation
Make some examples of the decorations described in 'What to do' and hang them up in one area of the setting.

What to do
Sit in the area where the decorations are displayed and play the chosen music. Invite the children to sit and look at them as they move gently in the air. Talk together about what you might see during winter, such as snowflakes and icicles and how these shimmer and shine especially as the light catches them. Explain to the children that they are going to make some more decorations based on winter shapes and colours.

Show the children the materials available and invite them to make their own decorations. Encourage the children to carefully cut out and decorate the card shapes with the shiny, glittery collage materials, decorating both sides. Give examples of other decorations that the children could make, such as:
◆ stars made from split pegs glued on to a disc of card, to form points, and then decorated with paint and glitter or
◆ snowflakes made by dipping cotton buds into glue and glitter and then placed into a circle of glue (the size of a 10p coin) on a piece of plastic. Leave to dry, then peel off.

Attach silver thread to all the decorations and hang around the setting.

Support and extension
Provide pre-cut card shapes for younger children to decorate. Invite older children to work together to make a mobile, hanging their shapes from a branch sprayed with white paint.

Home partnership
Ask parents and carers to donate suitable materials to use for the children to make the decorations.

Further ideas
◆ Make paper snowflakes from folded and cut paper.
◆ Print white handprints in a circle on blue paper and sprinkling with glitter while wet. Cut out to make snowflakes.
◆ Make a giant star, snowflake and icicle, decorated with 3-D collage in one colour such as silver for the star, white for the snowflake and clear materials on the icicle.

Theme links
Colours
Materials
Shapes

Brrr... it's cold!

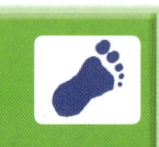
Group size
Four children.

What you need
Box; adult clothing such as hat, scarf, gloves, boots, jumper and jacket with different fastenings; four sets of the same clothing for children with different fastenings; four large dice; the photocopiable sheet 'Winter clothes' on page 96.

What to do

Place the clothes in the box and position it near the children. Talk about how people stay warm in winter when they are outside by dressing in warm clothing. Think of the different types and layers of clothes we wear and why we cover up our hands, necks and heads. Ask the children to help you get dressed for winter by singing the song 'This is the way we put on a...' to the tune of 'Here we go round the Mulberry Bush' and inviting a child in turn to take an item from the box. Look at the different fastenings on the clothing and ask the children to have a go at doing them up, helping them as appropriate. Talk about how warm and cosy you now are.

Invite the children to play 'Dressing for winter'. Explain that they need to collect clothing that has been scattered around the area to match the number rolled on a dice. Use the bottom half of the photocopiable sheet and write in numbers against each picture to decide which picture will correspond to the numbers on the dice. Ask the children to roll the dice in turn and collect the appropriate clothing. When all the clothing is collected encourage the children to have a go at putting on a set each, dressing themselves as independently as they can.

Use the top half of the sheet to give each child an 'I can put on...' certificate and ask them to colour in the pictures of the clothes they put on successfully.

Support and extension

For younger children not yet ready to use a number dice, play the game with a set of pictures fastened to the dice. Extend the activity by introducing a 'getting dressed' race to play in pairs, with one child finding the clothes for their partner to put on, the winner being the first pair to have a child dressed.

Home partnership

Send home the certificates showing the clothes the children put on independently.

Further ideas

♦ Place winter clothes in the role-play area.
♦ Set up a table with zips, buttons, rip fastening, buckles and poppers to investigate.
♦ Collect small baby clothes in which to dress teddies and dolls.

Theme links
Clothes
Ourselves
Weather

Swirling snowstorm

Group size
Small groups.

What you need
Examples of snowstorm toys; table; white sheet; small plastic jars with a screw top lid; plain materials to represent snow, such as coconut shreds, rice, plastic, white wool, string; silver, sparkly materials to represent frost, such as glitter, sequins, winter confetti, foil, shredded foil; glycerine; water; small plastic toys or cake decorations; strong glue; ribbon; small threadable bells.

Preparation
Place the white sheet on the table. Make a one-part glycerine to three-parts water mixture.

Stepping Stone
Use one object to represent another, even when the objects have few characteristics in common.

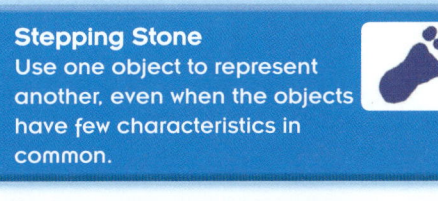

Early Learning Goal
Use their imagination in art and design, music, dance, imaginative and role play.

What to do
Place the snow shakers on the table and encourage the children to come and play with them. Talk about what happens when they are shaken and what they can see inside. Invite the children to make a winter snowstorm shaker of their own. Give each child a plastic jar and ask them to select and glue a decoration to the inside of the lid, setting it aside to dry overnight.

Examine the different materials and look at the difference between the plain and shiny ones. Ask, 'which would make the best snow?' and 'which the best ice shining in the sun?'. Invite the children to select a plain material for the snow and place a thin layer in the bottom of their jars, snipping it into tiny pieces if necessary. Next add 'frost' in the same way, snipping tiny pieces from the shredded foil or making tiny balls from the foil. Fill the jars with the glycerine-water mixture filling them nearly to the top and then securely screw on the lid.

Thread bells on to strips of ribbon and tie these around the neck of the jars. Shake the jars and watch the 'snow' swirling down.

Support and extension
Give hand-over-hand support where appropriate while younger children are making the shakers. Ask older children to experiment with the different 'snow' materials in water to decide which is the best one.

Home partnership
Invite parents and carers to lend you any unusual snowstorm shakers they have available for your display.

Further ideas
♦ Make miniature winter landscapes for small-world play using shaving foam or white play dough with glitter added.
♦ Decorate cakes and biscuits with white icing and add snowmen modelled from ready-to-roll icing. Dust with icing sugar snow.

Theme links
Snow
Toys

Foundation Themes
Seasons

Ice art

Stepping Stone
Use their bodies to explore texture and space.

Early Learning Goal
Explore colour, texture, shape, form and space in two or three dimensions.
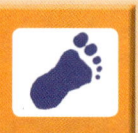

Group size
Small groups

What you need
Freezer; ice cubes; wide variety of materials (both manufactured and natural); sequins; pieces of winter plants, such as ivy; water; food colouring; ribbon; assorted tubs, lids and pots; adhesive tape; large deep trays.

What to do

Sit together and pass round some ice cubes for the children to examine and feel. Ask the children how they think the ice was made. Warn the children not to hold the cubes for too long to avoid hurting their fingers. Look at the beauty of an ice cube, holding it up to the light and finding the tiny trapped bubbles of air. Talk about how ice forms outside by water freezing when the weather is very cold. Explain to the children that they are going to make some very special winter works of art based on ice.

Show the children the materials and invite them to choose a container and to tape ribbon to the sides, so the ends are inside the container, forming a hanging loop. Fill with water, nearly to the top, adding a few drops of food colouring for coloured ice. Encourage the children to select from the different materials available and arrange them in the containers. Carefully place the containers in the freezer and leave until solid.

Release the ice from the moulds and hang up by a window with a tray underneath to catch the water. Watch the sculptures melting. Catch and feel the drips and items released and watch it change shape as it melts.

Support and extension

Let younger children work in pairs to support one another. Encourage older children to freeze orange slices and dried fruits in plain water. As they defrost, let them catch the drips on their tongues, and taste the fruit that has been set free.

Home partnership

Take photographs of each child's ice art. Frame them or make into cards or calendars to send home as a gift.

Further ideas

♦ Make winter feely pictures using bubble wrap snow, twig trees or snowflake confetti for the children to explore with their hands, while their eyes are closed.
♦ Make a large quantity of ice and use it to build 3-D sculptures; a little salt helps the pieces stick together.

Theme links
Changes
Ice
Shapes

Circle time

Circle-time activities are designed for the whole group, providing opportunities for the children to interact and to work as part of a team. The activities increase the children's ability to communicate effectively and to learn to share tasks.

Good growing

What to do

Read the story *The Tiny Seed* at the first circle time. It tells the story of a tiny seed blown a long way from the parent plant. Talk about how it needs fertile earth to grow until it too produces seeds which blow away. Talk about what might happen to these seeds and pass around the pots of seeds for the children to examine.

Encourage the children to talk about plants they have seen growing at home or in the setting. Ask them if they know how to care for plants. Explain that they will only grow if they have the right conditions and are well looked after with soil, light, warmth and water, which we have to give them if they are growing inside. Invite the children to grow some plants from seeds and care for them.

Place all the materials needed in the centre of the circle on a plastic sheet and help small groups of children to plant seeds in the plastic containers, inviting them to select which type of flower or vegetable seeds to plant. Show them how to place the compost and seeds in the lower part of the container, gently add water and put on the lid to make a 'greenhouse'. Discuss how to look after the seeds: giving them warmth, moisture and light as they start to grow. Give the groups responsibility for looking after their seeds and seedlings, planting them outside in pots when they are large enough.

Have regular circle times to share the progress of each group's seedlings and plants and enjoy another poem or story about growing seeds.

Further ideas

♦ Visit a garden centre and look at how plants are grown and cared for.
♦ Make up a play about a seed growing and add finger actions to accompany it.

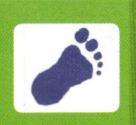

Stepping Stone
Display high levels of involvement in activities.

Early Learning Goal
Continue to be interested, excited and motivated to learn.

Summer skies

What you need
Large space; adult helpers; large blue sheet or piece of fabric with rounded-off corners; yellow ball with a bell inside (from a pet shop); cotton wool balls; white table tennis balls; CD player and CD with summertime sounds or music.

What to do
Sit in a circle and explain to the children that they are going to play a game based on summer skies. Spread out the blue sheet and ask them what it might represent, encouraging the answer 'the sky'. Invite the children to pull the 'sky' taut and as the music plays make it ripple by lifting it up and down. Next ask them to stand up and make a stormy summer sky, making it move quickly up and down.

Place the sheet back down on the ground and talk about what else is seen in a summer sky such as clouds, the sun and birds. Add the sun (a yellow ball) and invite the children to try to roll the 'sun' from side to side to each other without it rolling off, as the music plays in the background. Gently lower the sheet back to the ground and remove the ball.

Next, add the cotton wool clouds and ask the children to pick up the sheet carefully, without losing any clouds. Encourage gentle movements. Invite the children to slacken and pull the sheet taut to make the clouds bounce a little. Let the children try again with the table tennis balls, which requires more co-operation and gentler movements.

Further ideas
♦ Invite the children to make five or six birds from card and feathers and to fasten them to the underneath of the sheet with string and safety pins. Play games involving the sheet going high above heads to see the birds flying.
♦ Invite named children to run under the sheet as it is held taut in the air and swap places with each other.
♦ Pretend the sheet is the sea and repeat the games with plastic boats, foil fish and sea sounds or music.

Harvest time memory game

What you need
Selection of harvest foods such as fruit, vegetables, bread, jam, chutney, fruit cake, fruit juice; basket covered with a cloth; tablecloth.

What to do

Sit in a circle and explain to the children that they are going to play a harvest time memory game. Arrange the items on the tablecloth in the centre of the circle and help the children to name them. Ask each child to select an item from the cloth. Go round the circle and ask the child to describe something about the item they choose, for example a big green apple, a tiny brown potato, a soft white bread roll.

Next, pass the covered basket around the circle to each child in turn. Ask the first child to put in their item saying 'At harvest time I want to eat a… potato…'. Pass the basket on to the next child who says the phrase, their item and the name of the item from the previous child. For example 'At harvest time I want to eat a… cauliflower and a...potato…'. Encourage the children to think what each item is called and give clues to jog their memories if they forget. Invite children who cannot remember to have a look in the basket. Continue the game until everyone has had a turn.

Invite each children to select and help prepare an item of food to share at snack time. Talk to the children about what they are doing and introduce new vocabulary linked to that food, such as peel, skin, slice, pips, core if preparing apples.

After eating the food invite the children to play the memory game again, carefully selecting a food for them to describe, such as apples. Go around the circle saying 'I ate an apple and it was… sweet'. The next child then says, for example, 'I ate an apple and it was… green and sweet…'. Continue with other suggestions such as juicy, drippy or crunchy.

Further ideas

♦ Make up phrases and tongue twisters about the foods – enormous, orange pumpkins; crunchy, crinkly cabbages.
♦ Use the phrases that the children thought of in the activity above to make a harvest rhyme with a repeating chorus, inviting the children to place items in the basket as the rhyme is said.

Celebration bells

What you need
Music based on bells such as 'Wand of Youth' by Elgar (suite Number 2 – Little Bells); different types of bells (hand, wrist, sleigh, jingle, cow).

What to do

Sit in a small circle and invite the children to look at the different types of bells, passing them around and trying them out. Place the bells back in the centre of the circle. Talk about what a bell is, its unique shape and what the different types are for. Ask the children to think about when they have heard bells recently, for example from a place of worship for special winter celebrations and festivals, a clock chiming the time, or when listening to music and singing songs such as 'Jingle Bells' (Traditional). Explain that bells are sometimes rung when there is good news, by town criers who want everyone to stop and listen, and at the start of a new year to ring out the old year and ring in a new, good year.

Encourage everyone in the circle to think quietly for a short time of something good that has happened recently or some good news that they would like to share. Invite each person in turn to choose their favourite bell and ring it a few times before telling everyone their 'good news', replacing the bell carefully back in the circle afterwards. Encourage the other children to listen carefully and ask questions. As an alternative, the news givers could pretend to be town criers saying 'Hear ye, hear ye, hear ye. This is my good news today' before sharing it with the others in the circle, or start the sharing news time by singing Jingle bells, changing the last line to 'Oh what fun it is to share our news today'.

Finish by listening quietly to the music.

Further ideas

♦ Ask the children to write, or scribe their thoughts on to bell shaped paper. Add a decorated front and display them at child height.
♦ Paint pictures of special occasions when bells are rung, such as weddings and festivals.
♦ Place the bells on a table for the children to experiment with. Encourage them to find ways to muffle the sound.
♦ Find other musical instruments and objects that have a bell-like sound when struck.

Displays

This section gives suggestions for four interactive displays each one based on one of the four seasons. The displays link with activities in the main chapters.

Spring is here!

What to do

Cover the display board with blue backing paper. Invite the children to make 'height flowers' by helping each other to mark and cut a length of paper equal to their height and painting a large bright flower head at the top, with a thick stem to the bottom. Create a rainbow by making handprints in rainbow colour order. Cut out a card sun, clouds and raindrops and glue on collage materials to decorate. Make flowers such as daffodils (draw a star shape and add an egg-box cup, then paint it yellow) and bluebells (make two blue footprints and attach them to a stem). Staple the rainbow and sun on to the top part of the blue backing paper and the spring flowers below, along a border of grass cut from green backing paper. Secure the 'height flowers' to the wall, starting at floor level. Use Blu-Tack to secure the clouds and raindrops.

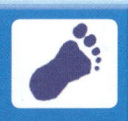

Stepping Stone
Begin to talk about the shapes of everyday objects.

Early Learning Goal
Use language such as 'circle' or 'bigger' to describe the shape and size of solids and flat shapes.

Using the display
♦ Look at the shapes of other flowers and make them from pre-selected resources.
♦ Make a hand pointer, fasten it on to the display and use it to indicate the weather.

Sunlight's colours

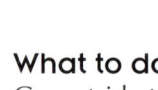
What you need
Display area (near a window); table; white backing paper; silver holographic gift bags and wrap; staple gun; string; white and coloured paper; red, yellow and blue paint; paintbrushes; tissue paper; PVA glue; A4 sheets of plastic; scissors; books, pictures and resources about rainbows, light and colour; bubble tubs; treasure chest; old CDs; light catchers; prisms.

What to do
Go outside together and ask the children to think about how bright and white the sunlight is in summer. Explain that it is a mix of different colours, which can be seen in a rainbow when the sun shines through raindrops, for example. Talk about how more rainbows occur in summer as there is more sunshine. Name the colours in a rainbow and show them to the children by blowing bubbles; invite them to investigate the colours.

Back inside, try colour mixing with groups of children. Show them how to make one red and one yellow handprint on white paper then how to rub both hands together and print with the colour that is made (orange). Repeat with the red and blue (purple) and then yellow and blue paint (green). Invite other children to mix two colours of paint in a palette and paint patterns with the colours made. Give the children circles cut from card and push a pencil through the centre to make spinners. Decorate them with paint, let them dry and then spin them, observing the colour made. Try with runny wet paint and watch the colours mix.

Cover the display board with the white paper and add a title and border from the gift wrap. Cut out any spare handprints and arrange these down two sides of the board. Finish the display by arranging the handprint pictures and patterns on the board, and the books, pictures, spinners and other resources on the table.

Hang the CDs, light catchers and strips of gift wrap in front of the window to catch the light and make rainbows. Place the treasure chest containing further CDs, light catchers and prisms near by.

Using the display
♦ Encourage the children to explore the effect of sunlight on the contents of the treasure chest, making and catching rainbows.
♦ Use the computer to write words to describe what the children discover in rainbow colours and display these alongside the items.
♦ Make a collection of items in the different rainbow colours and up-date or change it weekly.

Autumn leaves

Stepping Stone
Try to capture experiences and responses with music, dance, paint and other materials or words.

Early Learning Goal
Respond in a variety of ways to what they see, hear, smell, touch and feel.

What you need
Display board; table; hessian or taupe-coloured backing paper; orange fabric; border roll; staple gun; Blu-Tack; A3 pale coloured sugar paper; paint; paintbrushes; pastels; marker pens; wax crayons; glue; A3 card templates of common leaf shapes; scissors; books and pictures about autumn; copy of an autumn poem; natural items such as seeds, branches, bark and a large quantity of clean dry leaves.

What to do
Explain to the children that they are going to make an autumn display based on leaves. Go for a walk together and collect a wide range of leaves, observing the differences in colour, shape, size and feel. Ask each child to find one special leaf.

Invite groups of children to make paintings based on their special leaves, drawing around a template and carefully mixing paint to the correct colours. When these are dry encourage the children to add details and markings using pastels and marker pens. Finally, cut the leaves out.

Provide materials for the children to make representations of trees that they have seen on the walk, making a handprint with brown paint and adding finger dabs of paint for leaves.

Help the children to think of words to describe their leaves, writing these on to A3 card leaf shapes with marker pens, scribing if appropriate.

Ask the children to make leaf rubbings with wax crayons on to the border roll. Use other leaves and paint to make prints and cut them out when they are dry.

Cover the display board with hessian or taupe-coloured paper and add the border. Place the table in front, draping the fabric down one side. Arrange the painted leaves on and around the board, displaying the corresponding real leaves on the table and hanging some from a branch secured to the ceiling. Finish the display by arranging the leaf prints, a copy of the poem and the words on the leaf shapes on the board, and the natural items and books on the table.

Using the display
♦ Ask the children to sort the items on the table by texture such as rough or smooth, hard or soft and by colour.
♦ Place a branch with five leaves secured with Blu-Tack on the display table. Enact the song 'Five Little Leaves' in *This Little Puffin…* compiled by Elizabeth Matterson (Puffin Books).
♦ Place autumn treasure boxes containing 'autumn treasure' on the table and encourage the children to explore their contents.

Winter landscapes

What you need

Display board; table; pale coloured backing paper; silver border roll; lengths of blue fabric; staple gun (adult use); Blu-Tack; A3 pale coloured sugar paper in blues, white or grey; blue, white and black paint; paintbrushes; pastels; marker pens; salt; silver glitter; glue; square white paper; white wool; scissors; cling film; twigs sprayed white and silver; wellington boots; books and pictures about winter; copy of a winter poem; computer with WordArt package.

What to do

Cover the display board with the backing paper and add the border. Place the table in front. Drape the fabric down one side, twisting it together along the bottom and on to the table. Place the twigs on the table. Arrange the poem and pictures on the board. Show the children the display board and explain that they are going to make a winter display based on the poem.

Share the poem with the children and talk about the pictures and the colours that they can see. Talk about these colours being cold colours, evocative of winter. Invite groups of children to make paintings using these cold colours, some painting winter landscapes and others mixing different shades of paint and painting patterns. When the paintings are dry, invite the children to add details using white pastels and silver marker pens. Mount the patterns on to blue paper and add a window pane mount to the landscapes.

Help other children to make paper snowflakes by folding a paper circle into eight and cutting shapes from it with scissors. Open out, thread with white wool and attach these to the twigs and from the ceiling to make a flurry of snowflakes.

Invite the children to make prints with wellington boots and white paint and sprinkle these with salt while they are wet, then add a track of 'crystal' footprints to the display.

Finish the display with a large Jack Frost painted in cold colours mixed with salt and glitter and covered in a layer of cling film to represent the frost.

Using the display

◆ Make collections of objects in white, blue and silver colours evocative of winter.
◆ Think of some frosty words, write them with glue and sprinkle them with glitter and salt.
◆ Make masks by sticking glued tissue paper over one side of a balloon. Leave to dry, pop the balloon and decorate the masks. Create a Jack Frost dance to 'Winter' from *Four Seasons* by Vivaldi and display the masks.

Rhymes

Here comes the spring!

Out comes the sunshine
Down comes the rain
(throw arms open wide
move arms downwards wriggling fingers)

Up shoot the plants
In the fields again
(hands together point
and jump upwards)

Back come the birds
From far away
(flap arms
point away)

Out come the lambs
To skip and play
(throw arms open wide
skip in a small circle)

Down come the petals
From the blossom tree
(move arms downwards wriggling fingers
point arms up and out)

Here comes the spring
For you and me!
(make beckoning movement with both arms
point to others, then self)

Brenda Williams

Busy, busy, buzzing bee

Black and yellow, stripy bee
Making honey for my tea.

In and out of every flower
Busy, busy, every hour.

Buzzing, buzzing in the sun
Will his work be ever done?

To the hive to feed the queen
Round and round the leaves of green.

While you watch his beating wings
Don't forget that bees can sting!

Busy, busy, buzzing bee
Making honey for my tea.

Brenda Williams

Summer sunlight

Silver sun on rising
Golden when we play.
Yellow sunlight fading
At the end of day.

Blazing reds and orange
Fiery setting sun.
A sky of brilliant colours
When the day is done.

Brenda Williams

Where is squirrel?

(Tune: 'Pop goes the Weasel')

Why does squirrel run from me?
Where has squirrel run to?

Up a tree *(mime climbing, arms above head)*

With hippity-hop
Hiding from the raindrops. *(cover head with hands)*

Repeat replacing 'Up a tree' with the following:
Under leaves *(push one hand under the other)*
Inside pots *(make circle with fingers of one hand,*
push first finger of other hand inside)
Behind a log *(place one arm horizontally in front with fist clenched,*
push other hand behind it)
Beside a bush *(spread fingers of one hand vertically in front,*
place clenched fist of other hand next to it)
Between two trees *(show two fingers, place finger of other hand between them)*
In a puddle *(spread hand flat in front, jump other hand into it)*

(Invite the children to suggest other places and actions.)

Brenda Williams

Ten white snowmen

(Tune: 'Ten Green Bottles')

Ten white snowmen standing having fun
Ten white snowmen standing having fun

But when one white snowman melted in the sun
There were nine white snowmen standing in the sun.

Nine white snowmen standing having fun
Nine white snowmen standing having fun

But when one white snowman melted in the sun
There were eight white snowmen standing in the sun.

Eight white snowmen standing having fun... *(and so on)*

(Repeat, counting down to 'No white snowmen standing having fun!'.)

Brenda Williams

Sleepy, sleepy bear

Here comes winter when the snow falls deep
Here comes bear for his winter sleep
(repeat after each verse but last one)

Sleepy, sleepy squirrel hiding nuts near your tree
I need a cave all warm for me.

Sleepy, sleepy frog snuggled near your stream
I need a cave where I can dream.

Sleepy, sleepy hedgehog in your nest of grass
I need a cave till winter's passed.

Sleepy, sleepy snake in your rocky mound
I need a cave to be safe and sound.

Here comes a place with a cave that's deep
Sleepy, sleepy bear, have a long long sleep!

Brenda Williams

Songs

Please watch out!

(Tune: 'Frère Jacques')

Please watch out *(x2)*
For birds' eggs. *(x2)*
Nestled in their nests *(x2)*
Ready to hatch. *(x2)*

Please watch out *(x2)*
For shoots and buds. *(x2)*
They are busy growing *(x2)*
Into flowers. *(x2)*

Please watch out *(x2)*
For creatures small. *(x2)*
They have just been born *(x2)*
In the spring *(x2)*.

Sanchia Sewell

Ask the birds

(Tune: 'Mary, Mary, Quite Contrary')

Ask the birds that live all around us
How do you build your nest?
'We gather twigs and bits of grass
And weave them all together.' *(x2)*

Ask the birds that live all around us
How do you make it soft?
'We gather feathers, fluff and moss
And put them inside our nests.' *(x2)*

Ask the birds that live all around us
How do you make it safe?
'We hide our nests in the long grass
Or build them in the treetops.' *(x2)*

Sanchia Sewell

Foundation Themes
Seasons

The waves at the seaside

(Tune: 'To Market, to Market, to Buy a Fat Pig')

The waves at the seaside go crash on the rocks. *(clap on word 'crash')*
The tide at my feet murmurs splish-e-ty splosh. *(rub hands together)*
The seagulls are noisy as they swoop to the ground, *(swoop with hands)*
But the fish in the ocean don't make any sound. *(shake head, finger on lips)*

The shell at my ear whispers softly to me.
The water goes on as far as I can see.
In rock pools the water is gurgling free,
These are the sounds I hear close to the sea.

Sanchia Sewell

Did you ever see a spider?

(Tune: 'Did You Ever See a Lassie?')

Did you ever see a spider, a spider, a spider?
Did you ever see a spider
Spin a web out of silk?

The long threads go this way
And the short threads go that way.
And the longest thread of all goes round and round.

Did you ever... *(and so on)*

Spinning webs is very tricky
And she does it very quickly.
And then when the web is finished it will shine in the sun.

Sanchia Sewell

Apple song
(Tune: 'The Grand Old Duke of York')

There are apples you can munch
And apples you can crunch.
And apples you can cook and mash and give baby for lunch.

Some apples come in rings,
Some apples come in tins,
And sometimes apples lend their smell to candles, soap and things.

There are apples you can munch... *(and so on)*

Sanchia Sewell

Holly bushes lovely to see
(Tune: 'Baa Baa Black Sheep')

Holly bushes lovely to see
Careful they're quite prickly.
Shiny leaves stay green the whole year,
Bright red berries mean that winter is near.

Pine tree leaves are like needles or a pin,
Just as sharp and just as thin.
Pinecones lying on the ground,
Are bumpy, lumpy and woody brown.

Ivy leaves are green and white,
Sometimes dark and sometimes light.
Pointy edges on each leaf,
See it growing with a creep, creep, creep.

Sanchia Sewell

May flowers

SCHOLASTIC Photocopiable

Spring biscuits

Mix

Roll

Cut

Bake

Make your own garden

What does your finished garden look like?
Can you draw it?

What did you use?

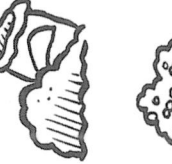 compost

 gravel

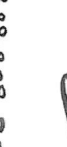 flower seeds

 grass seeds

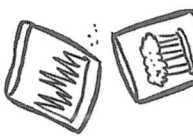 cress seeds

 little plants

 and a...

Beside the sea
Complete the pictures.

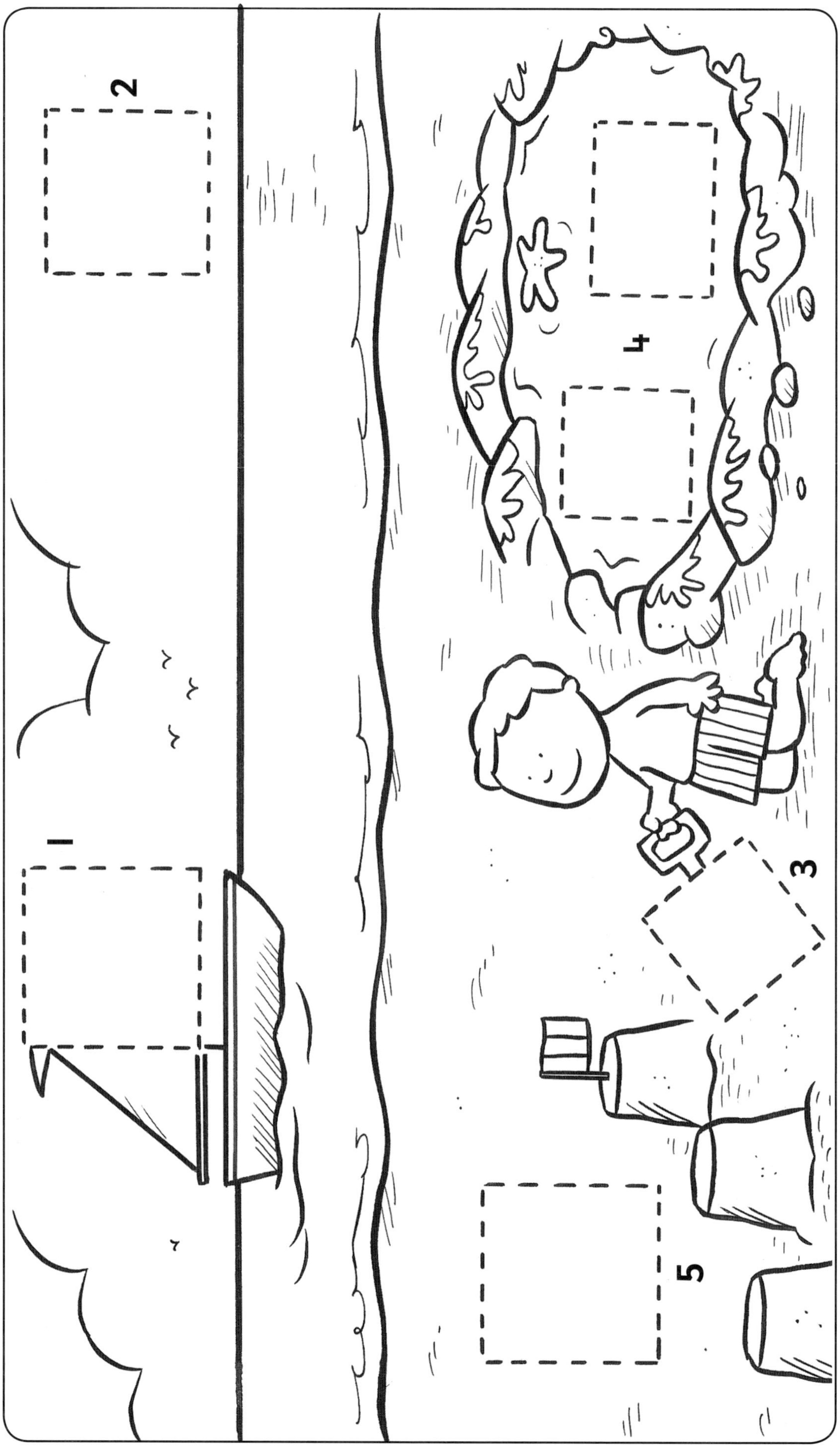

1

2

3

4

5

Apple tree bingo

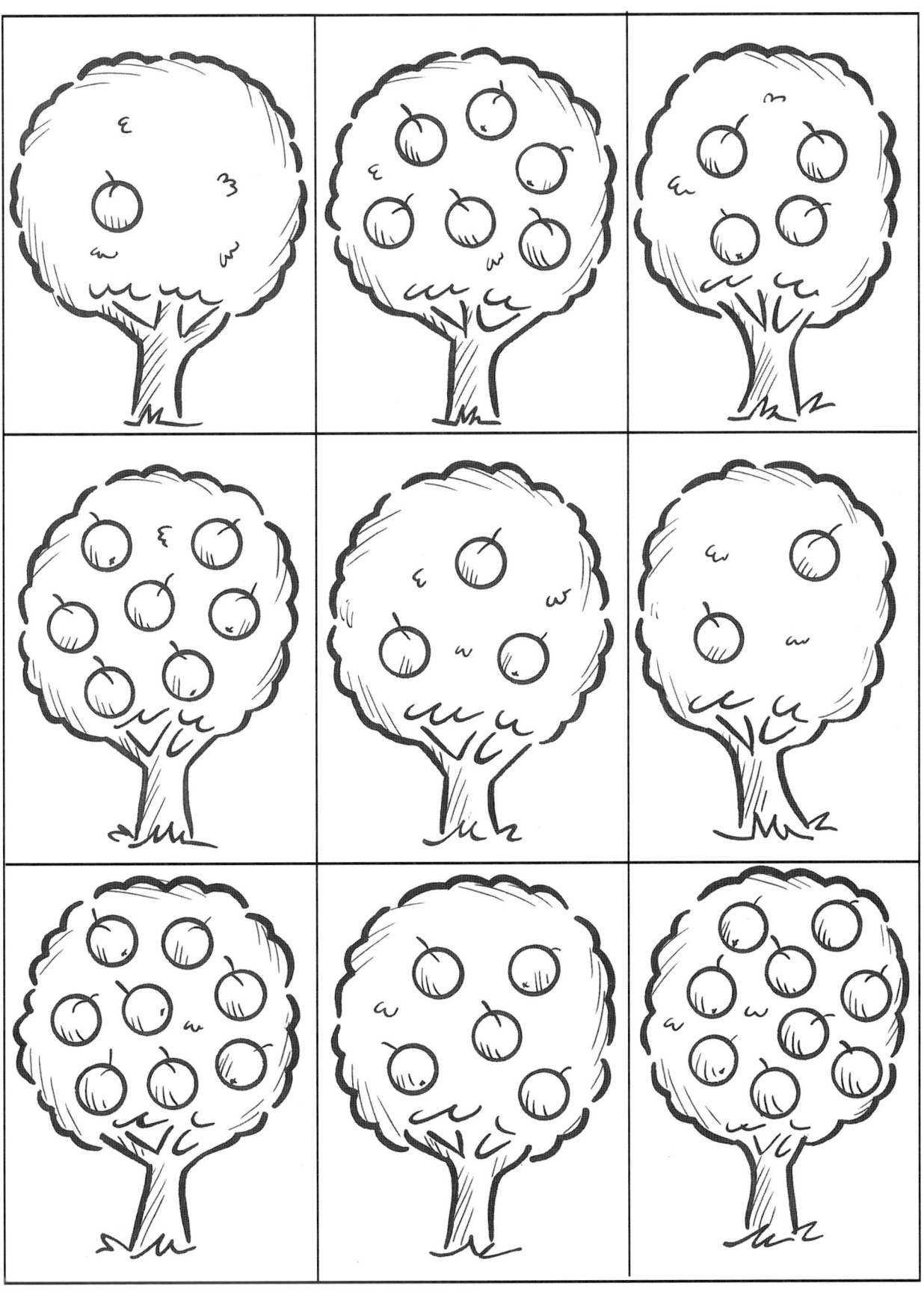

Treasure boxes

Winter shapes

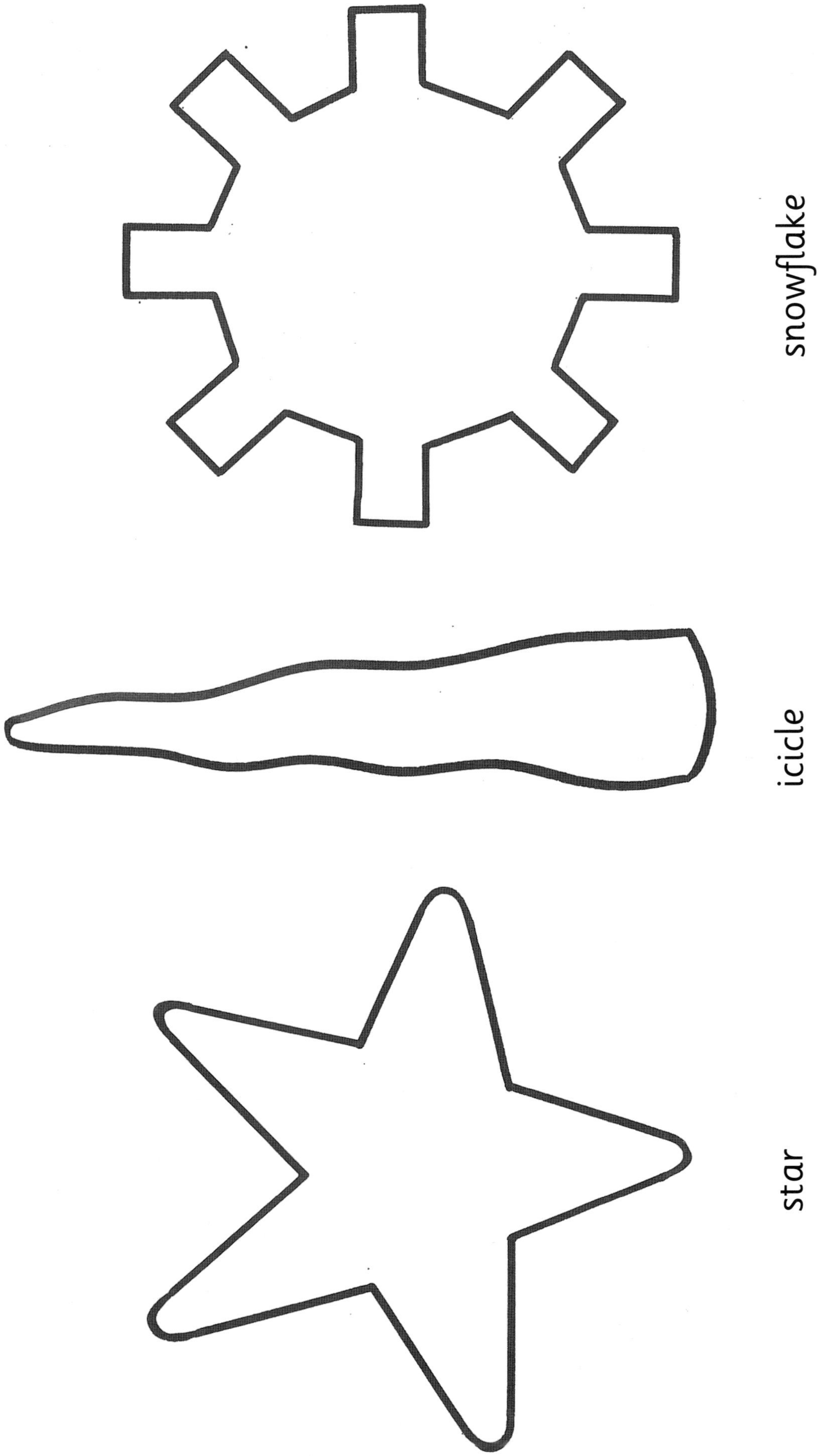

snowflake

icicle

star

Winter clothes

I can

hat

mittens

jumper

put on

gloves

coat

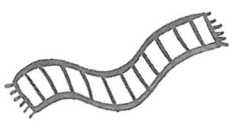

boots

scarf

What number?

hat

boots

jumper

mittens and gloves

coat

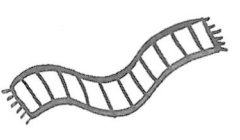

scarf